$10 MEALS
with Chelsea

Weekly meal plans
Tasty dinner recipes
Average $2.50 per serve

Chelsea Goodwin

Chelsea Goodwin is a recipe developer, home cook and single mother of three. Recognising how many people were struggling with the ever-rising cost of living, she created the popular $10 Meals Facebook communities to help Australians cook delicious meals on a very low budget.

Chelsea is passionate about sharing her love of cooking through her recipes and teaching basic cooking skills and meal planning principles, both online and in her local community of Brisbane.

She hopes to inspire households of all incomes and abilities to cook meals together from scratch, sample new cuisines and create lasting food memories around the table.

CONTENTS

Introduction

Who would have thought, two years ago, I would be writing a cookbook?

No one, that's who ... absolutely no one!

I'm not a chef. In fact, I've never even set foot inside a restaurant kitchen. It was only seven years ago that my passion for home cooking was sparked through binge-watching everyone's favourite domestic goddess on DVD (pre-streaming) in *Nigella Bites*.

At that point, I was a terrible cook. Really, really bad – just ask my kids!

Regardless, I cooked my way through Nigella's entire series and for the first time ever, experienced happiness, relaxation and pride in cooking for my family. From then, I wholeheartedly embraced cooking: learning to make delicious meals and treats by reading, watching, developing and testing recipes, on my journey to now – sharing my own ideas with you in my first cookbook.

Two years ago, I was (still am) a single mother of three, living week-to-week in the suburbs of Brisbane on a strict grocery budget of $150 a week to cover *all* of our food. I allocated $70 for dinner, leaving us $80 for breakfast, lunch and snacks. The biggest challenge was figuring out how to feed my family on such a low budget without compromising on flavour and variety.

For me, the obvious answer was meal planning. I began creating weekly plans for my family that were filled with delicious, nutritious meals – seven dinners for $70. Instead of Thai takeaway we'd have pad see ew for 'Fakeaway Friday' and if we wanted to enjoy meat, no worries, I'd find a way to stretch a larger cut over two or three meals. After some careful planning, creative thinking and cost-saving tweaks to my recipes, I couldn't believe we were able to eat so well on such a small budget! Better still, by batch-cooking, I was saving time too! I've now fully adopted budget meal planning and haven't looked back since.

One day, in August 2022, I decided to share one of my $10 meal plans on social media. The response was unexpected and completely overwhelming – in the best possible way.

I realised immediately that I had knowledge and resources I shouldn't gatekeep. The cost of living was rising rapidly and families were drowning under the pressure of trying to put food on the table. That same day, I created a free online community which grew in its first year to over 150,000 budget-conscious Australians.

I then threw myself into developing my recipes, regularly creating new $10 meal plans and sharing them with my community. In doing so, I discovered a genuine passion for inspiring and encouraging others to cook from scratch and spend less.

Some of you will be at the point I was at seven years ago – burning food and breaking the budget, where cooking is a chore and a stressor, just another duty you feel obligated to carry out in your role as parent, spouse or caretaker. Others may love to cook and be looking for some extra inspiration, especially during tougher times.

My hope is that the meal plans and recipes in this book will make your life a little easier in some way. Whether that's by taking a big chunk of stress out of planning and cooking, helping you find your cooking mojo or reducing your grocery spend.

This book is a complete budget dinner solution. If you've been relying on meal kits, frozen meals or takeaway, it's time to ditch them! I've created 10 weeks of dinner plans and affordable grocery lists that include many ingredients you may already have. Now, all you need to do is check off the items you have, add the rest to your shopping list, and *get cooking!* It couldn't be easier (or quicker!).

It would bring me an immense amount of joy to know that this book has had a positive impact on you. So don't be a stranger, reach out to me through my website or join one of my $10 meal communities online. I'd love to hear about your cooking journey!

Chelsea

How to Use This Book

I wrote this book to be a practical resource. I want to save you the time and effort of having to put together your own budget meal plans and shopping lists, so you can focus on cooking delicious meals and spending time with the people you care about.

In this book you'll find 10 chapters, each containing:

- a weekly meal plan with seven dinners
- a comprehensive guide for each day of the week
- a grocery list with every item you'll need
- options for ingredient substitutions based on cost, seasonality or dietary requirements
- detailed, tested recipes with loads of tips
- photos for every recipe.

Here's where I suggest you start

1. **Read the rest of this section!** The most important info you need is right here. I want to ensure that you're getting the most out of this book and have the greatest chance of success with my recipes.

2. **Review the Equipment and Pantry lists** (see pages 9 and 11). You'll need some basic cooking equipment and ingredients to get started. With your pantry, the more staples you have the less it will cost you to cook each week's plan. Don't worry if you're low on these though – you can build them up slowly over time as you need them.

3. **Find a comfy seat, grab a tea or coffee** (or a wine, whatever works!) and flip through the plans and recipes. Choose one plan to start with – whichever has recipes that are most appealing to you! If you can't decide, start with Week 1.

4. **Figure out what you need to get started.** Tick off what you already have in the grocery list and make a shopping list of what you need. Make sure you stock your shelves with enough time to prepare for the week ahead.

So you're ready to start cooking? Let's talk about the recipes!

In the kitchen

First, a couple of quick technical things to note before you cook anything from this book.

All of the temperatures listed are for a fan-forced oven. If you cook using a conventional oven (no fan) adjust the oven temperature to 20°C higher than the listed temperature.

I use 15 ml tablespoons in my recipes. A standard Australian tablespoon is 20 ml but many sold in shops here are 15 ml (so confusing!). Check which one you have and keep this in mind or you may end up with imbalanced flavours. It won't make much difference to 4-serve meals, but if you make double quantities of a recipe, it could. If things get out of whack, use my Recipe Rescue tips (page 12) to help save the day.

Recipe layout

It was really important to me that this book is an inclusive book that can be used by, and is useful for everyone. Whether you're the beginner cook, the 11-year-old cook, the neurodivergent cook or the time-poor cook – I want you to succeed with my recipes and be proud of the meals you create.

So I've done things a little differently!

You'll see that in each recipe, I've separated the method into two separate sections: Prep and Cook. There's a few reasons for this:

1. It's not as easy as celebrity chefs make out to cook and prep at the same time without burning the food!

2. When you're making any fast-cooking recipe, like a stir-fry, you really do need to prep in advance!

3. I want to give you the option of prepping earlier in the day or handing off those tasks to someone else (kids, partner, housemate, etc.).

4. I've had lots of feedback from people with additional needs (and lived experience as a mother of a teen with ASD/ADHD who loves to cook) that clear, simple prep instructions are essential.

Servings

Each recipe yields a minimum of 4 servings. In my home I'm feeding a family of four – me and three teenagers – so they're always adult-sized servings.

For the recipes that serve 5 or 6, you'll be given options for the leftovers. Where the recipes yield 8 servings, there will be a 'leftover night' in the meal plan so you can take a night off cooking and reheat the remainder of the meal.

At the start of each chapter, I've listed the total number of servings for that week. This number refers to the number of whole meals. I haven't included any side dish recipes/servings.

Cost

Not every recipe in this book is a '$10 meal' – I want to make that very clear! In order to create budget meal plans with variety and super delicious recipes, I always have a mix of lower cost dishes that supplement the higher cost meals in that plan. I also keep costs down by sharing ingredients between recipes in any given week. My budget for dinners per week for my family of four is $70, so when averaged out across the week the seven dinners equate to $10 each.

I've listed the cost per serving of each meal plan which I've capped for each plan at $2.50 per serve or under. This is based on prices in the major supermarkets at the time of writing in 2023.

In calculating the costs for each recipe/meal plan I have included the full cost of any ingredient not included in the pantry list. For items on the pantry list (sauces, flour, spices etc), I've calculated the cost per unit and applied that to the quantity used for each recipe.

Tips

At the bottom of each recipe you'll find plenty of tips from me to you which I hope will help answer any questions that aren't covered in the recipe instructions. I've given instructions for leftovers, timing, substitutions and ways to boost the flavour or decrease the heat (because not everyone loves chilli as much as I do!).

Dietary substitutions

Use the tags (below) in addition to the notes in the ingredients and the tips below the recipes to check whether a recipe is suitable for your particular dietary requirements. A large proportion of the recipes are either gluten-free, dairy-free or easily adapted to be so. There are meat-free recipes in almost all of the meal plans and, in most cases, those that aren't can be adjusted to be vegetarian or vegan. Alternatives for a range of ingredients are offered in the notes that open each weekly chapter.

Tags

I've added bold, colourful tags to each recipe so you can easily identify whether it can be adapted to your dietary requirements, is freezable, or quick to prepare.

 Fast – on the table in less than 30 minutes.

 Freezable – read the 'leftovers' instructions in recipe notes.

 One pot – cooked in one pot, save on washing up!

 Dairy-free – completely free of dairy.

 Dairy-free option – can be made dairy-free by following recipe notes.

 Gluten-free – completely free of gluten.

 Gluten-free option – can be made gluten-free by following recipe notes.

 Vegetarian – completely meat-free.

 Vegetarian option – can be made vegetarian by following recipe notes.

My Top 5 Tips for Cooking Success

1. Read the recipe (and notes) *before* you start cooking

Taking 5 minutes to read through the recipe before you cook can save a lot of time (and frustration) later on. I also recommend adding an extra 5 to 10 minutes to the prep and cook time if you're trying a recipe for the first time.

2. Safety first

A sharp knife and stable cutting board are essential. If you can't afford to lose a finger, then you can't afford to compromise on safety! Keep your knives sharp and pop a damp tea towel or paper towel underneath your cutting board to stabilise it.

3. Embrace the 'trash bowl'

From one messy cook to another, trust me when I say that using a 'trash bowl' has changed the way I prep and clean. Take any medium-sized bowl, set it next to your chopping board and dump all the scraps into it as you go. If you compost or save scraps for stock, use two bowls – one for regular trash, another for green waste. When you're finished prepping, simply dump your scraps into the bin, making clean-up a breeze!

4. Taste and season, taste and season, taste and season . . .

Some of us like salty food or spicy food and some of us prefer more subtle flavours. You need to taste and season throughout the cooking process to create a dish that's perfectly seasoned to *your* taste. On that note, please be aware that unless needed as a specific ingredient, I haven't listed salt or pepper when it's used for seasoning. Seasoning is entirely dependent on taste – some of you will use it to season every dish, others of you might prefer to avoid using salt for health reasons. Most chefs apply salt liberally and pepper occasionally. As you develop your own cooking preferences, let taste be your guide, tasting and adjusting as you go.

I always have salt and pepper handy whenever I am preparing, cooking and serving meals. I'm also a fan of cooking in salted water, especially starchy ingredients like potatoes and pasta that soak up the flavour. When you see instructions to 'put a large pot of salted water on to boil', simply add 1 tablespoon of salt for pasta or 2 tablespoons for potatoes to a large pot of water and set it to boil.

5. Make it your own

Take notes and scribble down any substitutions, additions or changes that you make and love. I want these recipes to become yours.

What to Use When

Even the most basic ingredients can become confusing when there are so many varieties to choose from. What's the difference between crushed garlic, garlic powder or that stuff that comes in the jar, for example, not to mention all the different types of rice, mustards, salts ... the list goes on!

Let me introduce you to the four ingredients I'm quizzed on most often and which you'll be reaching for time and again.

Ingredient	Used for	Substitute with
OIL		
Extra virgin olive oil	A deep-coloured, intense-flavoured oil best used for salad dressing, drizzling, dips and low-heat cooking.	Grapeseed oil, macadamia oil or light olive oil.
Olive oil	All the heart-smart benefits of extra virgin olive oil without the robust flavour. Best for all-purpose and general cooking.	Vegetable oil, avocado oil or grapeseed oil.
Vegetable oil	Ideal for high-heat cooking such as stir fries, deep frying and baking.	Peanut oil for stir fries, and canola oil or sunflower oil for deep frying or baking.
SALT		
Table salt	Finer grains that don't clump together due to the addition of anti-caking agent – often sold in a pouring container. Best for baking and general cooking.	Cooking salt.
Cooking salt	Medium-sized grains that occasionally clump together – typically sold in bags that you spoon from. Best for savoury dishes and all-purpose cooking.	Table salt.
Sea salt	Sold as salt flakes or rocks that need grinding. Best used to finish meals or season salads, meat or vegetables.	Himalayan pink salt.
RICE		
Basmati rice	A lean, long grain that retains its structure when cooked, with a nutty, savoury flavour. Used in Indian, Middle Eastern and African dishes to make flavoured rice dishes such as pilaf/pilau and biryani, and to accompany curries and stews.	Any long-grain rice.
Jasmine rice	A sweeter, more fragrant flavour that cooks to a light, fluffy and slightly sticky texture. Most often used in South-east Asian cuisine.	Either long-grain or short-grain white rice, depending on dish.
Medium-grain rice	Neutral grain in size, flavour and composition. Good all-rounder that works with any meal, used to make flavoured rice dishes such as paella and pilaf.	Depending on your cuisine, look to replace with basmati, jasmine or a short-grain rice.

Ingredient	Used for	Substitute with
Arborio rice	Short-grain rice used in cooking Italian dishes such as risotto, arancini and rice pudding.	Bomba or medium-grain rice.
Bomba rice	Short-grain rice used in Spanish meals such as paella.	Arborio or medium-grain rice.
Sushi rice	Short-grain rice used in Japanese cuisine.	There's really no ideal substitute for this highly absorbent, sticky rice.

GARLIC

Ingredient	Used for	Substitute with
Garlic powder (dried, in a jar)	Best in sauces, spice mixes, savoury cooked dishes – its texture is easily absorbed.	1 garlic clove = ⅛ teaspoon.
Garlic granules (dried, in a jar)	Dry rubs, soups – adds texture and flavour.	1 garlic clove = ¼ teaspoon.
Garlic cloves (fresh)	Crushed or finely diced. Always the best choice unless you need a dry variety for a rub or spice mix.	½ teaspoon minced garlic in a jar, 1 teaspoon garlic paste, ⅛ teaspoon garlic powder, ½ teaspoon garlic granules.
Minced garlic (fresh, in a jar)	Best in cooked dishes when time is of the essence.	1 garlic clove = ½ teaspoon.

Equipment List

This is a complete list of the equipment you'll need to cook every recipe in this book.

I've tried to keep things simple because you really don't need expensive appliances or fancy gadgets to cook great-tasting food.

Most of these items should be familiar to you and hopefully already have a home in your kitchen!

Essential equipment

- chef's knife
- paring knife
- bread knife
- 2 cutting boards
- vegetable peeler
- garlic crusher
- box grater
- zester/microplane
- can opener
- citrus juicer
- tongs
- whisk
- ladle
- masher
- slotted spoon
- measuring cups
- measuring spoons
- small, medium and large mixing bowls
- colander
- fine-mesh sieve
- large stockpot with lid
- large frypan
- medium saucepan with lid
- large baking dish
- large deep roasting tray
- shallow baking tray
- 12-cup muffin pan
- stick blender
- plastic wrap
- alfoil
- baking paper
- paper towel
- tea towel
- oven mitts

Nice to have . . . but not essential

- slow cooker
- large wok
- cast-iron French pan
- food scraper
- kitchen scissors
- digital thermometer
- kitchen scales

Pantry Staples

The recipes in this book have been developed around this core list of pantry staples. If you were to purchase this list in its entirety at the major supermarkets, you should be able to stock your pantry for just over $100.

Start by checking off the items you already have and adding more each week as you need them. If your budget allows, I recommend keeping your pantry permanently stocked with these staples so you can always whip up tasty, home-cooked meals.

Seasonings

- salt (table or cooking)
- pepper (ground black)
- whole peppercorns (for grinder)
- garlic powder
- paprika
- ground turmeric
- dried oregano
- dried chilli flakes
- cayenne pepper
- ground cumin
- ground cinnamon
- ground coriander

Asian sauces

- light soy sauce
- dark soy sauce
- oyster sauce
- sesame oil
- fish sauce
- sriracha
- rice wine vinegar

Pantry

- cooking oil spray
- extra virgin olive oil
- olive oil
- vegetable oil
- white vinegar
- jasmine rice
- basmati rice
- panko breadcrumbs
- sesame seeds
- honey
- tomato paste
- mayonnaise
- cornflour
- polenta
- plain flour
- self-raising flour
- baking powder
- bicarb soda
- caster sugar
- brown sugar
- chicken stock cubes/powder
- vegetable stock cubes/powder
- beef stock cubes/powder

Fridge

- eggs
- unsalted butter
- milk
- parmesan
- plain Greek yoghurt

Recipe Rescue

Help! What to do when your dish hasn't turned out quite right.

We all have stuff-ups and they're more likely to occur when you're cooking a new recipe for the very first time. These are my go-to solutions for common cooking problems that can leave you feeling frustrated in the kitchen.

Before you declare your dish a 'fail' and start ordering takeaway, give these tried-and-tested quick fixes a go. I've listed them in the order that I would attempt them, but use common sense when deciding which one would best suit the recipe that you're attempting to rescue.

Also, although the recipes in this book have been tested multiple times to ensure success, you might ultimately prefer more salty, sweet or spicy flavours than me. Use the suggestions below to guide your adjustments. Don't be afraid to scribble your notes on the recipe page itself, so you can recreate it exactly the way you like it next time.

Too salty

- Add water.
- Add acid – a squeeze of lemon, lime or vinegar.
- Add sugar or something sweet.
- Add fresh tomatoes or tinned tomatoes.
- Add extra veg or carbs.

Too sweet

- Add acid – a squeeze of lemon, lime or vinegar.
- Add spice – cayenne pepper (¼ teaspoon at a time), a pinch of dried chilli flakes, sriracha or chilli paste.

Too sour/acidic

- Add sugar or something sweet.
- Add a pinch of bicarb soda.

Too spicy

- Add fat – milk, sour cream, cream, mayonnaise or yoghurt.
- Add sugar or something sweet.
- Add water or stock.

Too bland

- Add salt.
- Add pepper.
- Add a crumbled stock cube.
- Add fresh herbs.
- Add a squeeze of lemon or lime, or a splash of vinegar.
- Add spice – dried or fresh chilli.

Too runny

- Make a cornflour slurry – mix 1 tablespoon cornflour + 1 tablespoon water into a paste then stir into the sauce to thicken.
- Let the sauce simmer, uncovered, until it reduces and thickens.
- Remove and blend some of the vegetables in the dish, then add them back in to thicken the sauce.

—

Fan Favourites

Week 1

Sunday
Mexican Beef Chilli

Monday
Rainbow Minestrone

Tuesday
Beef Chilli Mac 'n' Cheese

Wednesday
Greek Lemon Chicken and Potatoes with Spanakorizo

Thursday
Rainbow Minestrone

Friday
Loaded Potatoes

Saturday
Chicken Soup

Week 1 at a Glance

★ **28 meals**
plus 2 leftovers

★ **$2.47**
per serving

This week's meal plan is my most cooked, most shared, most loved plan. It's the one I come back to when I'm craving simple comfort food.

All of these dishes are guest-worthy and most can be easily adapted to cater for dairy-free and gluten-free diets.

Our hero dish is the **Mexican Beef Chilli** which we'll serve in three meals: first with rice, then in **Beef Chilli Mac 'n' Cheese** and finally, as a topper for **Loaded Potatoes**. You'll have a night off cooking on Thursday night – just heat up your leftover **Rainbow Minestrone** and serve with a hunk of crusty garlic bread or a cheese toastie.

Sunday

This **Mexican Beef Chilli** recipe yields enough for 8 servings over rice but will stretch to 12 in this meal plan as you'll use smaller quantities for the **Beef Chilli Mac 'n' Cheese** and the **Loaded Potatoes**. For a family of 4, serve about half of the batch for tonight's dinner (with **Cornbread Muffins**), freeze 2 cups for Friday's **Loaded Potatoes** (defrost overnight Thursday) and store the remainder (approximately 2–3 cups) in the fridge for Tuesday's **Beef Chilli Mac 'n' Cheese**.

Monday

This **Rainbow Minestrone** will be on regular rotation in your home if you love it as much as my family does! This recipe makes 8 servings but if you're not going to eat it all this week, store your leftovers in the freezer – it's just as delicious when defrosted and even yummier with garlic bread.

Tuesday

My **Beef Chilli Mac 'n' Cheese** is a tray of carby cheesy comfort and it's just so simple to make. It can stretch to 5 or 6 servings, but only if you can restrain yourself from eating seconds!

Wednesday

Greek Lemon Chicken and Potatoes is my favourite dish from this week's plan. I always serve it with **Spanakorizo** (spinach rice) and so can you, using the leftover silverbeet, lemon, garlic, some onion and a few pantry staples.

Thursday

Tonight you'll reheat leftovers from Monday's **Rainbow Minestrone**. For something different, I usually serve it up the second night with a cheese toastie. Don't forget to defrost the **Mexican Beef Chilli** for tomorrow night!

Friday

For Fakeaway Friday, we're making **Loaded Potatoes** topped with **Mexican Beef Chilli**. Use whatever you have available to top the potatoes, but from this week's grocery list you'll have cheese and sour cream, plus the chilli beef. Sweet potatoes work just as well, if you have some on hand.

Saturday

This **Chicken Soup** is my go-to for flu season. You can add in some grated fresh ginger with the garlic for an extra zingy 'wellness boost'. You'll appreciate having leftovers which can be frozen or reheated. For an alternative, check out the recipe notes, as this dish can be transformed into creamy Avgolemono (Greek Egg and Lemon Soup) with just one additional step.

Week 1 Grocery List

Ingredients in italics are Pantry Staples (page 11), so you may have them already.

Meat and Fish

- 2 kg chicken drumsticks (12)
- 1 kg beef mince

Fruit and Veg

- 2 kg all-purpose potatoes
- 1 bunch rainbow silverbeet
- 5 brown onions
- 3 bulbs garlic
- 5 carrots
- 1 bunch celery
- 1 red capsicum
- 1 bunch flat-leaf parsley
- 5 lemons
- 1 jalapeño

Fridge and Freezer

- sour cream
- 250 g tasty cheese
- 100 g feta
- *2 eggs*
- *unsalted butter*
- *milk*
- *parmesan*

Pantry

- 3 × 800 g tins diced or crushed tomatoes
- 2 × 400 g tins kidney beans
- 1 × 400 g tin cannellini beans
- 1 × 400 g tin corn kernels
- 500 g macaroni
- 1 baguette/French bread stick
- *olive oil*
- *salt*
- *pepper*
- *paprika*
- *ground cumin*
- *dried oregano*
- *dried chilli flakes*
- *cayenne pepper*
- *beef stock cubes/powder*
- *chicken stock cubes/powder*
- *vegetable stock cubes/powder*
- *tomato paste*
- *basmati rice*
- *polenta*
- *plain flour*
- *caster sugar*
- *honey*
- *baking powder*

Week 1 Swap 'n' Save

Some weeks the budget is tighter than others, or you're more busy, more tired, have unexpected guests, want to mix things up or are catering for dietary preferences. Use the tips below to vary your recipes accordingly.

⊙ Swap out

chicken drumsticks → bone-in chicken thigh cutlets

rainbow silverbeet → regular silverbeet

kidney beans → black beans

basmati rice → long-grain rice

tasty cheese → cheddar or colby cheese

tinned corn → frozen corn

macaroni → any small pasta shape

⊛ Pocket some savings

Stock: All these recipes can be made using stock cubes or powder without compromising flavour. Powders are generally the most economical, with prices as low as 10 cents per litre compared to liquid stock which can cost upwards of $2 per litre.

Buy in bulk: Buying a bag of carrots, lemons and brown onions may be cheaper than buying these items individually. Always compare the prices.

Mince: 3- or 4-star beef mince has the optimal fat content for the **Mexican Beef Chilli**. Don't pay the premium for extra-lean mince unless you're consciously limiting your fat intake.

⊟ Leftover ingredients

You may have leftover sour cream this week, especially if you've bought a new tub. Here's what you can do with it:

- Use it for **Beef Burrito Bowls, Chicken Paprikash** or **Beef 'n' Bean Nachos** (Week 5).
- Mix it with mayo and whip up a potato or pasta salad dressing.
- Add it into baked goods or pancakes.
- Swirl it through your **Roasted Pumpkin Soup** (Week 6).
- *Freeze it!* It won't retain its silky texture when defrosted but it's perfect to use in baked goods or any recipes where it's cooked.

Mexican Beef Chilli

A hearty party in your mouth

SERVES 12 (4 for this meal,
4 each in 2 other meals this week)
PREP 15 minutes
COOK 50 minutes

4 cloves garlic, crushed
1 large brown onion, diced
3 stalks celery, diced
1 red capsicum, diced
1 tablespoon paprika
1 tablespoon ground cumin
½–1 teaspoon cayenne pepper
2 teaspoons dried oregano
1 teaspoon salt
400 g tin corn kernels, drained
2 ½ tablespoons olive oil
1 kg beef mince
3 tablespoons tomato paste
2 × 800 g tins diced or crushed
   tomatoes
2 beef stock cubes
2 × 400 g tins kidney beans, rinsed
   and drained

To serve
steamed basmati rice
sour cream
Cornbread Muffins (page 23)
parsley, finely chopped

PREP

✓ Crush the garlic and dice the onion, celery and capsicum.

✓ Combine the paprika, cumin, cayenne pepper, oregano and salt in a small bowl and set aside.

✓ Reserve half the corn for the topping and the other half for the **Cornbread Muffins**.

COOK

1. Heat 2 tablespoons oil in a deep pan or pot over medium heat, then add the onion. Cook for 3–4 minutes, stirring occasionally, until soft. Add the celery and capsicum and cook for another 2 minutes. Add garlic and cook for another minute, stirring to ensure the garlic doesn't burn. Add the combined spices and salt to the pan. Stir through and cook for 1 minute.

2. Turn the heat up to medium-high then add the beef mince. Cook for about 5 minutes, breaking it up and continually stirring until it's mostly browned. Add the tomato paste, tomatoes and 1 cup (250 ml) water, then crumble in the stock cubes. Stir together and bring to a simmer.

3. Turn the heat down to low, add the kidney beans then let it simmer gently with a lid on for 20 minutes (this is a good time to start cooking your rice).

4. Remove the lid, stir well then season with salt and pepper to taste. Let it simmer for 5–10 minutes uncovered, until thickened slightly.

5. Meanwhile, make the charred corn topping. Heat remaining oil in a small frying pan over medium-high heat. Add the reserved corn and cook, stirring, until it chars. Season with salt and pepper.

6. Serve the beef chilli over steamed rice. Top with the charred corn and a dollop of sour cream.

NOTES

Dairy-free: Leave off the sour cream.

Leftovers: Tastes even better the next day! Store for 3 days in the fridge, 3 months in the freezer. Reheat in the microwave or on the stovetop.

Meal plan: If cooking as part of the meal plan, reserve 2 ½ cups for the **Beef Chilli Mac 'n' Cheese** and 2 cups for the **Loaded Potatoes**.

Spice level: For mild spice, start with ½ teaspoon cayenne pepper. I'm a spice fiend and will usually add 1 to 2 teaspoons.

Substitutions: You can use a combination of 50/50 pork and beef mince. Tinned black beans can be used in place of the kidney beans.

Cornbread Muffins

Just the right blend of sweet and savoury

SERVES 12
PREP 10 minutes
COOK 20 minutes

125 g unsalted butter, melted
   and cooled
1¼ cups (185 g) plain flour
¾ cup (125 g) polenta
¼ cup (55 g) caster sugar
1 tablespoon baking powder
1 teaspoon salt
¾ cup (180 ml) milk
2 eggs, beaten
1½ tablespoons honey
200 g corn kernels, drained

To serve
butter

PREP

✓ Preheat oven to 160°C.

✓ Melt the butter and set it aside to cool.

✓ Spray a 12-cup muffin pan with baking spray or lightly grease with oil.

COOK

1. In a large bowl, whisk or stir together the flour, polenta, sugar, baking powder and salt.

2. Make a well in the middle and add the milk, eggs and honey. Whisk or stir until just blended then add melted butter and corn. Fold gently to combine and don't worry if there are some small lumps.

3. Spoon the batter evenly into the muffin pan, filling each cup about two-thirds full.

4. Bake for 18–20 minutes or until the edges are light golden brown.

5. Cool in the pan for at least 5 minutes then gently remove. Serve warm as is, or halve and spread liberally with butter.

NOTES

Credit: I have been cooking these for years after finding Jenn Segal's recipe on her blog, *Once Upon a Chef*. I have made a few changes but this still remains quite true to her incredible recipe.

Leftovers: Store in a container in the fridge for 2 days or in the freezer for up to 2 months. Reheat by wrapping in foil and heating in the oven for 10 minutes.

Rainbow Minestrone

Chunky, colourful and packed with goodness

SERVES 8
PREP 15 minutes
COOK 40 minutes

4 cloves garlic, crushed
2 brown onions, diced
3 large carrots, diced
3 stalks celery, diced
2 tablespoons finely chopped flat-leaf parsley leaves, plus extra to serve
1½ cups (150 g) sliced silverbeet stems
2 cups (60 g) sliced silverbeet leaves
400 g tin cannellini beans, rinsed and drained
2 tablespoons olive oil
1 teaspoon salt
1 tablespoon dried oregano
½ teaspoon dried chilli flakes
3 tablespoons tomato paste
800 g tin diced or crushed tomatoes
8 cups (2 litres) vegetable or beef stock
1 cup (125 g) macaroni

Garlic bread
1 baguette
125 g unsalted butter, softened
3 cloves garlic, crushed
1 tablespoon finely chopped flat-leaf parsley leaves
½ teaspoon salt

To serve
juice of ½ lemon
crumbled feta or shaved parmesan

PREP

✓ Crush the garlic, dice the onion, carrots and celery and finely chop the parsley.

✓ Slice the silverbeet stems (below the leaves) into thin crescents then gently tear the silverbeet leaves away from the stems and slice the leaves into very thin shreds, discarding that part of the stem.

✓ Drain and rinse the cannellini beans.

COOK

1. Heat the oil in a large pot over medium-low heat then add onion and cook gently for 4–5 minutes, until soft. Add carrot and celery and cook, stirring occasionally, for another 5 minutes. Add garlic and cook, stirring, for another minute.

2. Add salt, oregano, chilli flakes and tomato paste and stir to combine. Cook for a couple of minutes then add the tomatoes, stock and 2 cups (500 ml) water. Increase the heat to medium-high and bring to the boil, stirring occasionally. Keep an eye on it, and as soon as it comes to the boil, reduce to medium-low again so it simmers. If you have the time, leave it simmering, partially covered with a lid, for 5–10 minutes.

3. While the soup is simmering, to make the **garlic bread**, slice the baguette diagonally into 2–3 cm slices and combine the butter, garlic, parsley and salt in a bowl. Smear the garlic butter over the cut side of the baguette, arrange on a baking tray and set aside.

4. About 10 minutes before you're ready to serve, remove the lid and add the silverbeet stems and macaroni. Return to a simmer and cook for 5 minutes, until macaroni is almost cooked. Preheat the grill in your oven. Add silverbeet leaves, cannellini beans and parsley to the soup, and cook for a further 5 minutes, until heated through and macaroni is tender. Season with salt and pepper to taste.

5. Pop the garlic bread under the grill for a couple of minutes or until lightly browned. Ladle the soup into bowls. Squeeze some lemon juice into each bowl and top with the extra parsley, and either feta or parmesan. Serve with the garlic bread.

NOTES

Dietaries: For dairy-free, omit the feta or parmesan. For gluten-free, use gluten-free pasta or omit the pasta and add an additional tin of cannellini beans and serve with gluten-free bread. For vegetarian, use vegetable stock and leave off the cheese too, for vegan.

Leftovers: Store in the fridge for up to 4 days, or up to 3 months in the freezer.

Reheat in the microwave or on the stovetop.

Meal plan: You'll use about half a bunch of the silverbeet leaves for this recipe and store the remainder for the **Spanakorizo** on Wednesday.

Meat-lovers: I often use 200 g chopped bacon or chorizo to enhance the flavour. I like to cook it in the oil before the onion, on medium-high heat, then remove it, leaving the delicious, fatty juices in the pan. I then lower the heat and carry on from step 1, adding the meat back in the final 10 minutes along with the macaroni.

Stock: If you're not cooking vegetarian, beef stock really adds depth of flavour. Chicken could also be used.

Beef Chilli Mac 'n' Cheese

Always a big hit with the kids!

SERVES 6
PREP 5 minutes
COOK 20 minutes

2 ½ cups (200 g) grated tasty cheese
3 cups (375 g) macaroni
2 ½ cups leftover **Mexican Beef Chilli** (page 20)

To serve
sour cream
½ jalapeño chilli, thinly sliced

PREP

✓ Preheat oven to 190°C. Bring a large pot of salted water to the boil over high heat.

✓ Grate the cheese, set aside.

COOK

1. Add the macaroni to the boiling water and cook until barely al dente, about a minute or two less than packet directions.

2. While the macaroni is cooking, heat the **Mexican Beef Chilli** in a large ovenproof pan over low heat, stirring occasionally. If it sticks to the pan, add a tablespoon of water at a time until it is a little saucier.

3. When the macaroni is ready, scoop out 1 cup of the pasta water (for later) then drain the macaroni in a colander.

4. Add about ¼ cup (60 ml) of the pasta water to the beef chilli in the pan and stir it through. Gently tip the macaroni into the pan and stir to combine. You can add a little more pasta water if it is too thick to handle easily. Turn off the heat (remove to another unused hob if you can). Add 1 cup (100 g) grated cheese and stir through carefully until melted. Taste and season with salt and pepper if you like.

5. Switch your oven to the grill setting. Use the back of a large spoon to even out the macaroni mixture in the pan. Sprinkle the remaining grated cheese over the top then carefully transfer the pan to a rack in the top half of the oven.

6. Cook for about 5 minutes, keeping a close eye on it to ensure that the cheese doesn't burn, until you have a melted, golden cheese topping.

7. Serve with a dollop of sour cream and the jalapeño.

NOTES

Gluten-free: Use gluten-free pasta.

Leftovers: Store this in the fridge for up to 2 days or the freezer for up to 1 month. Reheat in the microwave, or in the oven in a foil-covered ovenproof dish.

Pan: I use a cast iron French pan or an ovenproof sauté pan, with a minimum 3 litre capacity. If you don't own something similar, just use a large frypan then transfer the mixture into a baking dish to grill the cheese.

Greek Lemon Chicken and Potatoes

For those who love lemon as much as I do

SERVES 4
PREP 15 minutes + marinating time
COOK 45 minutes

¼ cup (60 ml) olive oil
¼ cup (60 ml) lemon juice
    (about 2 large lemons)
3 cloves garlic, crushed
1 tablespoon dried oregano
2 teaspoons salt
¼ teaspoon ground black pepper
⅛ teaspoon cayenne pepper (optional)
8 chicken drumsticks (about 1.5 kg)
1 kg potatoes
½ cup (125 ml) chicken stock

To serve
1–2 tablespoons finely chopped
    flat-leaf parsley leaves
2–3 tablespoons crumbled Greek feta
Spanakorizo (page 30)

PREP ▶

✓ Preheat oven to 200°C.

✓ In a bowl large enough to fit all the chicken, mix the oil, lemon juice, garlic, oregano, salt, pepper and cayenne pepper (if using) together until combined.

✓ Add the chicken to this mixture, turning to ensure every piece is well coated. Stand at room temperature while you peel the potatoes and cut them into thin wedges. (If you like, you can marinate the chicken a day ahead. Cover bowl and refrigerate until cooking time.)

✓ Peel potatoes and slice into thin wedges.

COOK ▶

1. Remove the marinated chicken drumsticks from the bowl with tongs and place in a large baking dish, leaving the excess marinade in the bowl.

2. Tip the potatoes into the bowl and coat well with the remaining marinade. Arrange the potato in the baking dish with the chicken, in a single layer. Season with a bit more salt and pepper.

3. There should still be a little marinade left in the bowl. Add the chicken stock to the remaining marinade and pour it carefully into the corner of the baking dish, making sure that it goes underneath the chicken and potatoes (so it doesn't wash off the marinade).

4. Bake on the middle shelf in the oven for 40–45 minutes, until tender and cooked through. If you like, turn on the grill setting for 5 minutes at the end to brown the top, but keep a close eye on it!

5. Sprinkle with parsley, and the crumbled feta. Don't throw out the pan juices because they're delicious and can be poured over the chicken and potatoes. Serve with **Spanakorizo** or your choice of side dish.

NOTES

Baking dish: If you prefer that all of the potatoes are crispy, you'll need to bake them in a single layer. If you don't own a dish large enough for this, separate the chicken and potatoes into 2 baking dishes and add an extra ⅓ cup (80 ml) stock to each baking dish.

Dairy-free: Omit the feta.

Leftovers: Store in the fridge for up to 2 days or the freezer for up to 3 months. Reheat in the microwave, or in the oven in a foil-covered ovenproof dish.

Meal plan: If you're making the **Spanakorizo**, start the prep about 15 minutes after you put the chicken in the oven.

Substitutions: Skin-on, bone-in chicken thighs or marylands can be used instead of drumsticks.

Spanakorizo (Spinach Rice)

My family's favourite rice dish!

SERVES 4–6
PREP 10 minutes
COOK 25 minutes

½ brown onion, finely diced
2 cloves garlic, crushed
3 cups (90 g) finely shredded silverbeet
2 tablespoons olive oil
1 teaspoon salt
1½ cups (300 g) basmati rice, rinsed
3 cups (750 ml) vegetable
    or chicken stock

To serve
2 tablespoons finely chopped flat-leaf
    parsley leaves
2 tablespoons crumbled feta
juice of ½ lemon

PREP

✔ Dice the onion, crush the garlic and finely shred the silverbeet.

✔ Rinse the basmati rice well in a large metal sieve.

COOK

1. Heat oil in a medium saucepan on medium-low heat and gently cook onions for a few minutes until translucent.

2. Add garlic and silverbeet and stir until wilted.

3. Add salt, rice and stock and stir gently together until well incorporated.

4. Bring to the boil then turn down heat to lowest setting. Cook with the lid on for 15 minutes.

5. Turn the heat off and leave to steam for another 5 minutes or until rice is tender.

6. Transfer to a serving dish, sprinkle with parsley and feta, and drizzle with lemon juice.

NOTES

Dairy-free: Omit the feta.

Meal plan: When I cook this with the **Greek Lemon Chicken and Potatoes**, I scoop out a tablespoon or so of the chicken's lemony pan juices and trickle it over the rice for extra flavour.

Silverbeet: If you find that you have less than 3 cups of silverbeet leaves remaining after cooking the minestrone soup, don't worry. Even with 1½–2 cups of leaves, it will still be delicious.

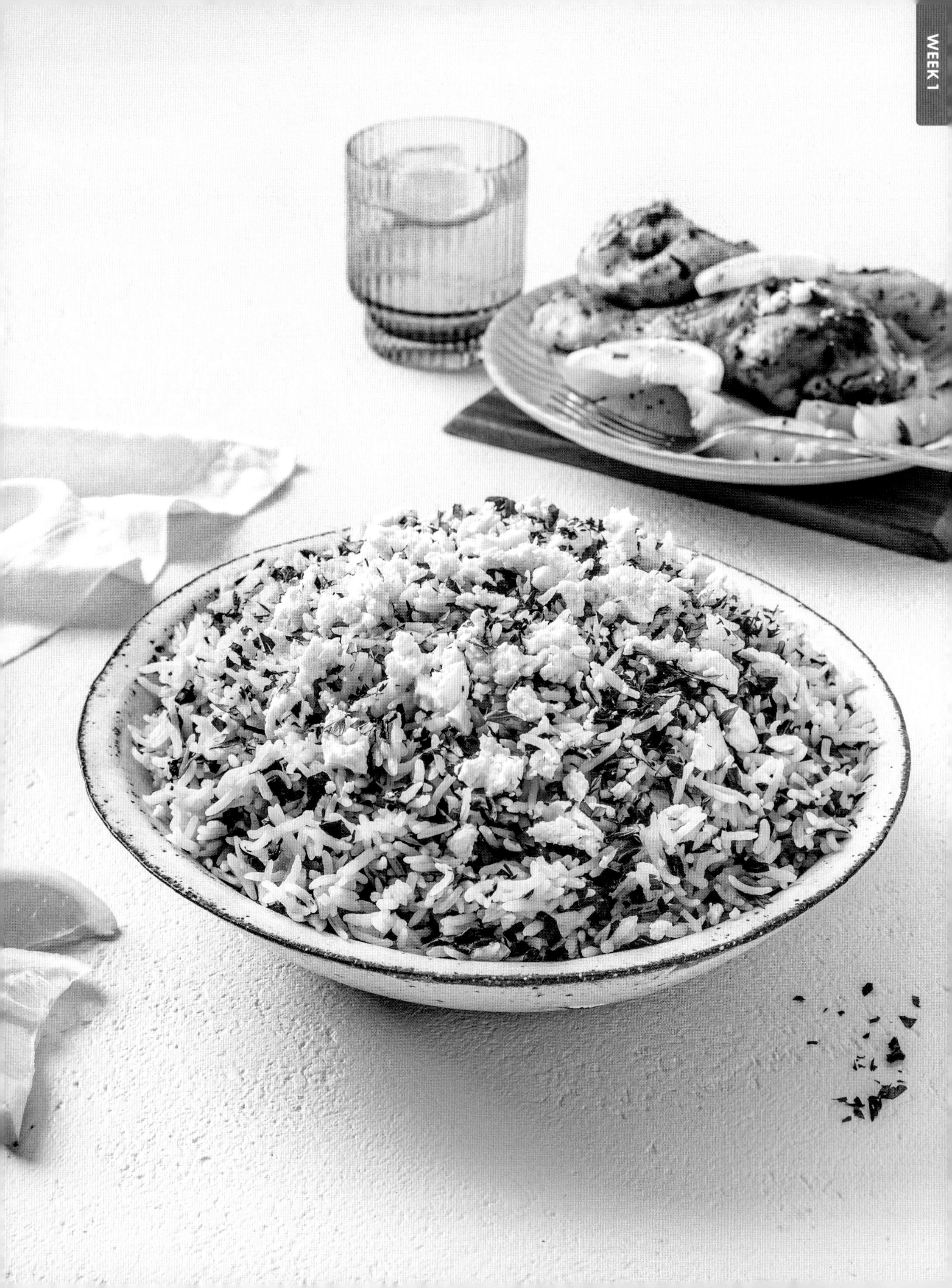

Loaded Potatoes

Crispy on the outside, fluffy on the inside

SERVES 4
PREP 10 minutes
COOK 1 hour 15 minutes

1 kg potatoes
1–2 tablespoons olive oil
1–2 teaspoons salt
2 cups leftover **Mexican Beef Chilli**
(page 20)
½ cup (50 g) grated tasty cheese

To serve
sour cream
½ jalapeño chilli, finely diced

PREP

✔ Preheat oven to 200°C. Line an oven tray with baking paper.

✔ Wash potatoes and dry well with a tea towel or paper towel (don't peel!).

COOK

1. Use a fork to lightly poke holes in each potato 5 or 6 times. Place the potatoes on the lined tray. Rub (or brush) the skin all over with a light covering of olive oil then sprinkle with salt.

2. Place tray on a rack in the middle of the oven and bake the potatoes for 60–75 minutes. The cooking time will depend on the size of the potato. The skin should be pretty crispy and you should be able to easily pierce the potatoes with a skewer or a knife. If in doubt, cook for another 5–10 minutes.

3. Just prior to removing the potatoes from the oven, heat up the **Mexican Beef Chilli** (on the stovetop or in the microwave) and prepare any additional toppings (see Notes).

4. Carefully slice the potatoes from end to end, making sure that you don't cut all the way down to the bottom. You can use a fork to gently fluff up the insides if you wish.

5. Spoon the beef chilli onto each potato, sprinkle with grated cheese and top with a generous dollop of sour cream. Top with the finely diced jalapeño.

NOTES

Leftovers: There probably won't be any, but if you have leftover baked potatoes, you can store them in the fridge for up to 3 days. Reheat in the oven at 180°C for 15–20 minutes.

Potatoes: When choosing potatoes go for all-rounders or a variety that is labelled as suitable for baking. You can serve 1 large potato or 2 smaller ones per person, but try to choose similar-sized potatoes so they cook at the same time.

Toppings: My personal preference is to put a good dollop of butter (which melts) on the potato after I've fluffed it up. I then season it again with salt and pepper before adding the beef chilli, cheese and sour cream. If you have spring onion or coriander, sprinkle it over the top for extra colour and flavour.

Chicken Soup

Wellness boost in a bowl

SERVES 4–5
PREP 10 minutes
COOK 1 hr 10 minutes

1 brown onion, diced
2 carrots, diced
2 stalks celery, thinly sliced
3 cloves garlic, crushed
1 tablespoon olive oil
1 teaspoon dried oregano
8 cups (2 litres) chicken stock
4 chicken drumsticks
½ cup (100 g) basmati rice
1 lemon, halved

To serve
2 tablespoons chopped flat-leaf
   parsley leaves

PREP

✓ Dice the onion, carrot and celery and crush the garlic.

COOK

1. Heat the oil in a large pot over medium-low heat. Add the onion and cook gently for 2 minutes. Add carrot and celery and cook for another 3–4 minutes, stirring occasionally, until soft. Add garlic and cook, stirring, for 1 minute. Stir in the oregano, stock and 2 cups (500 ml) water, then add the chicken.

2. Bring to the boil, then reduce heat to low and simmer, covered, for at least 50 minutes, until the chicken meat starts to come away from the bone.

3. Transfer chicken to a large shallow bowl. Use 2 forks to pull the chicken meat off the bone and tear into shreds. Return meat to the pan and add the rice. Cook for another 10 minutes, or until the rice is tender.

4. Skim any fat from the surface. I usually get at least ¼ cup (60 ml) out because I like a clearer soup. Taste and season with salt and pepper.

5. Ladle the soup into bowls. Squeeze some lemon juice into each bowl and top with the parsley.

NOTES

Avgolemono: You can transform this into a creamy Avgolemono (Greek Egg and Lemon Soup) after skimming off the fat. Just whisk ½ cup (125 ml) fresh lemon juice and 2 eggs together in a medium bowl. Use a ladle to add 1 to 2 large scoops of the soup (mainly the stock) into the egg and lemon mixture. This tempers the eggs so they don't scramble. Stir together gently, then pour the mixture into the soup pot.

Leftovers: Store in the fridge for up to 2 days or the freezer for up to 3 months. Reheat in the microwave or on the stovetop.

Substitutions: You can use shredded cooked roast chicken, sliced raw chicken breast or chicken thigh fillets for this recipe. Just add in with the stock and reduce the simmering time to as little as 15 minutes for roast chook or 20 minutes for raw breast or thighs.

Flavour Bombs

Week 2

Sunday

Vietnamese Meatballs with Asian Slaw

Monday

Zingy Chicken Tray Bake

Tuesday

Meatball Bánh Mì

Wednesday

Buttermilk Fried Chicken

Thursday

Vegetable Massaman Curry

Friday

Pork Noodle Stir-Fry

Saturday

Vegetable Massaman Curry

Week 2 at a Glance

 **28 meals**
plus 2 leftovers

 **$2.43**
per serving

We start off the week by batch-cooking **Vietnamese Meatballs**. The mixture will be the base of three recipes this week, all of which deliver with big flavours and can be prepared in under 30 minutes. For those who don't eat pork, don't worry, I've got you! Just substitute the pork for chicken mince. It's just as tasty and wallet-friendly.

Sunday

The **Vietnamese Meatball** mixture is so easy to prepare. Just remember to reserve and freeze a third of the raw mix (about 2 cups) for the **Pork Noodle Stir-Fry** on Friday night. The rest will be rolled into meatballs and cooked tonight. Of those, you'll serve half tonight with steamed rice, dipping sauce and **Asian Slaw**. The rest you'll save in the fridge for Tuesday's **Meatball Bánh Mì**. In preparation for tomorrow night's dinner, marinate the chicken.

Monday

The flavours in tonight's **Zingy Chicken Tray Bake** will take you on a quick trip to Mexico. For those among us who are coriander-averse, as per the recipe notes, you can leave it off as it's still very yummy without. Ideally, you'll marinate the chicken overnight or from this morning. However, you can get away with marinating for 20–30 minutes if you're short on time.

Tuesday

This **Meatball Bánh Mì** (Vietnamese roll) is the perfect light meal to pack up and take to evening sports training or alternatively, makes a great lunch box option. Serve as is or bulk up the meal by serving with rice or a salad.

Wednesday

The only problem with this **Buttermilk Fried Chicken** is that it's so good, you'll wish you doubled the recipe! You'll have about 1 kg of potatoes and 250 g of green beans from the Grocery List to use for side dishes. I usually serve this meal with mashed potato or potato salad and some steamed or roasted green beans. You might prefer a green salad depending on the season. Any leftover chicken can be used in wraps or salads for lunches the next day.

Thursday

You'll make a double batch of this **Vegetable Massaman Curry** which will feed your family tonight and Saturday night. To make Saturday night super-easy, make a double batch of rice too, then just reheat your meal in the microwave. This recipe can be easily adapted for meat lovers by adding in chicken (see recipe notes). Pull the meatball mixture out of the freezer and let it defrost overnight in the fridge, ready for tomorrow's dinner.

Friday

For Fakeaway Friday, it's a **Pork Noodle Stir-Fry** using the remainder of the meatball mixture already infused with so much flavour. It will be ready in around 25 minutes, depending on how quickly you can prep those veggies. It makes about 6 serves but don't count on there being leftovers if your family enjoys it as much as mine does!

Saturday

Tonight you can take a break from cooking because you're just reheating the **Vegetable Massaman Curry** and rice. Put your feet up!

Week 2 Grocery List

Ingredients in italics are Pantry Staples (page 11), so you may have them already.

Meat and Fish

- 1.5 kg pork mince
- 800 g (4 large) skin-on, bone-in chicken thigh cutlets
- 800 g chicken tenderloins or breast fillet

Fruit and Veg

- 2 kg all-purpose potatoes
- 1 bunch green onions
- 1 red onion
- 1 brown onion
- 2 bulbs garlic
- 30 g fresh ginger
- 2 kg carrots
- 1 kg sweet potatoes
- 750 g green beans
- 1 red cabbage
- 1 large bunch coriander
- 1 continental cucumber
- 2 red capsicums
- 3 limes

Fridge and Freezer

- *milk*
- *unsalted butter*

Pantry

- 4 Vietnamese bread rolls
- 3 × 400 g tins coconut cream
- 2 × 400 g packs shelf-fresh hokkien noodles
- 2 × 114 g tins Maesri massaman curry paste
- *vegetable oil*
- *olive oil*
- *salt*
- *pepper*
- *paprika*
- *garlic powder*
- *ground cumin*
- *dried oregano*
- *cayenne pepper*
- *brown sugar*
- *caster sugar*
- *jasmine rice*
- *plain flour*
- *baking powder*
- *white vinegar*
- *rice wine vinegar*
- *mayonnaise*
- *light soy sauce*
- *dark soy sauce*
- *oyster sauce*
- *sriracha*
- *fish sauce*
- *cornflour*
- *chicken stock cubes/powder*
- *beef stock cubes/powder*

Week 2 Swap 'n' Save

Some weeks the budget is tighter than others, or you're more busy, more tired, have unexpected guests, want to mix things up, or are catering for dietary preferences. Use the tips below to vary your week accordingly.

➡ Swap out

coconut cream ⟶ coconut milk

red cabbage ⟶ wombok cabbage

chicken breast ⟶ chicken tenderloins

pork mince ⟶ chicken mince

chicken thigh cutlets ⟶ chicken drumsticks

Vietnamese bread rolls ⟶ baguette (cut into 15 cm lengths)

fresh coriander ⟶ fresh mint

Ⓢ Pocket some savings

Cabbage/wombok: If these are not available or too expensive, it may be cheaper to purchase a 500 g bag of coleslaw which can be used for both the **Asian Slaw** and **Pork Noodle Stir-Fry**.

Chicken: If you have the knife skills, you can joint a small chicken for the tray bake. Buying a whole chicken generally works out cheaper than buying chicken cuts – you can use the remaining chicken in other dishes and use the carcass to make homemade stock.

Coconut cream/milk: Home-brand is generally half the price of premium brands.

Curry paste: Maesri Thai curry pastes can be purchased at Woolworths and on Amazon for around $2 per tin. You can use other brands, but the flavour and level of heat varies so the amount you use in the recipe will also vary.

Noodles: Dry egg noodles may be a cheaper alternative than fresh hokkien noodles. I have used shelf-fresh hokkien noodles, dry egg noodles, fresh chow mein noodles and even instant noodles for Friday's stir-fry. The 800 g weight is for fresh noodles only. If purchasing uncooked (dry) noodles you'll only need about 400 g.

Pork mince: Save up to $3 per kg by choosing regular pork mince rather than lean or extra lean. A little extra fat is always welcome in meatball recipes to ensure that they stay soft and don't dry out.

◯ Leftovers

If you cook the recipes as written, you shouldn't have any leftover ingredients, aside from your pantry staples. You will, however, have two extra serves of **Buttermilk Fried Chicken** to use for lunches or snacks (that is assuming you don't eat it all for Wednesday night's dinner, which is very possible!).

Vietnamese Meatballs

The crowd favourite you have to try

1.5 kg pork mince
⅓ cup (75 g) brown sugar
6 green onions, pale parts finely
   chopped (reserve dark parts
   for garnish)
¼ cup coriander leaves, finely chopped
6 cloves garlic, crushed
2 teaspoons finely grated fresh ginger
4 ½ tablespoons fish sauce
1 ½ teaspoons salt
¾ teaspoon ground black pepper
¼ cup (60 ml) vegetable oil

Dipping sauce
2 tablespoons caster sugar
1 ½ tablespoons fish sauce
½ teaspoon sriracha
1 small clove garlic, crushed
juice of ½ lime

To serve
steamed jasmine rice
½ continental cucumber, thinly sliced
Asian Slaw (page 45)
1 reserved green onion dark part,
   thinly sliced
coriander leaves
lime wedges

PREP

✓ Combine the pork mince, brown sugar, green onion, coriander, garlic, ginger, fish sauce, salt and pepper in a large mixing bowl. Mix well with a large spoon for a couple of minutes, and don't be afraid to use your hands (gloves optional!).

✓ If following the meal plan, reserve a third of the mixture and store (uncooked) in a container in the freezer for Friday's **Pork Noodle Stir-Fry**.

✓ Roll 1 ½ tablespoons of the remaining mixture into meatballs. You can keep them as rounds or flatten them down a little like tiny patties. If making ahead, store in the fridge, covered, for up to 24 hours.

✓ For the **dipping sauce**, combine the sugar, fish sauce, sriracha, garlic, lime juice and 2 tablespoons water in a small bowl. Set aside or refrigerate until ready to serve.

COOK

1. Heat the oil in a large frying pan over medium-high heat. Cook meatballs in batches for about 7–8 minutes, turning occasionally, until browned all over and cooked through.

2. Serve 4–5 meatballs per person in a bowl with steamed rice, cucumber and **Asian Slaw**. (The remaining meatballs will be used for Tuesday's **Meatball Bánh Mì**.)

3. Drizzle the dipping sauce over the rice and meatballs and top with sliced green onion, coriander and lime wedges.

NOTES

Leftovers: The meatballs can be frozen (raw or cooked) for up to 3 months. Store in the fridge for up to 3 days and reheat in the microwave or in the oven, in a covered ovenproof dish.

Meal Plan: Set aside at least 4 cooked meatballs per person if making the **Meatball Bánh Mì**.

Spice: For a spicy kick, add up to 1 tablespoon of sriracha to the meatball mixture.

Substitutions: If substituting pork mince with chicken mince, you will most likely need to add breadcrumbs to bind the meatballs. Start with ¼ cup (25 g) and keep adding until the meatballs bind together. Coriander can be substituted with fresh mint.

Timing: If serving with steamed rice, start the rice while you're prepping the meatballs and it should be ready at the same time. I recommend cooking 2 cups (400 g) rice, which will yield 6 cups cooked.

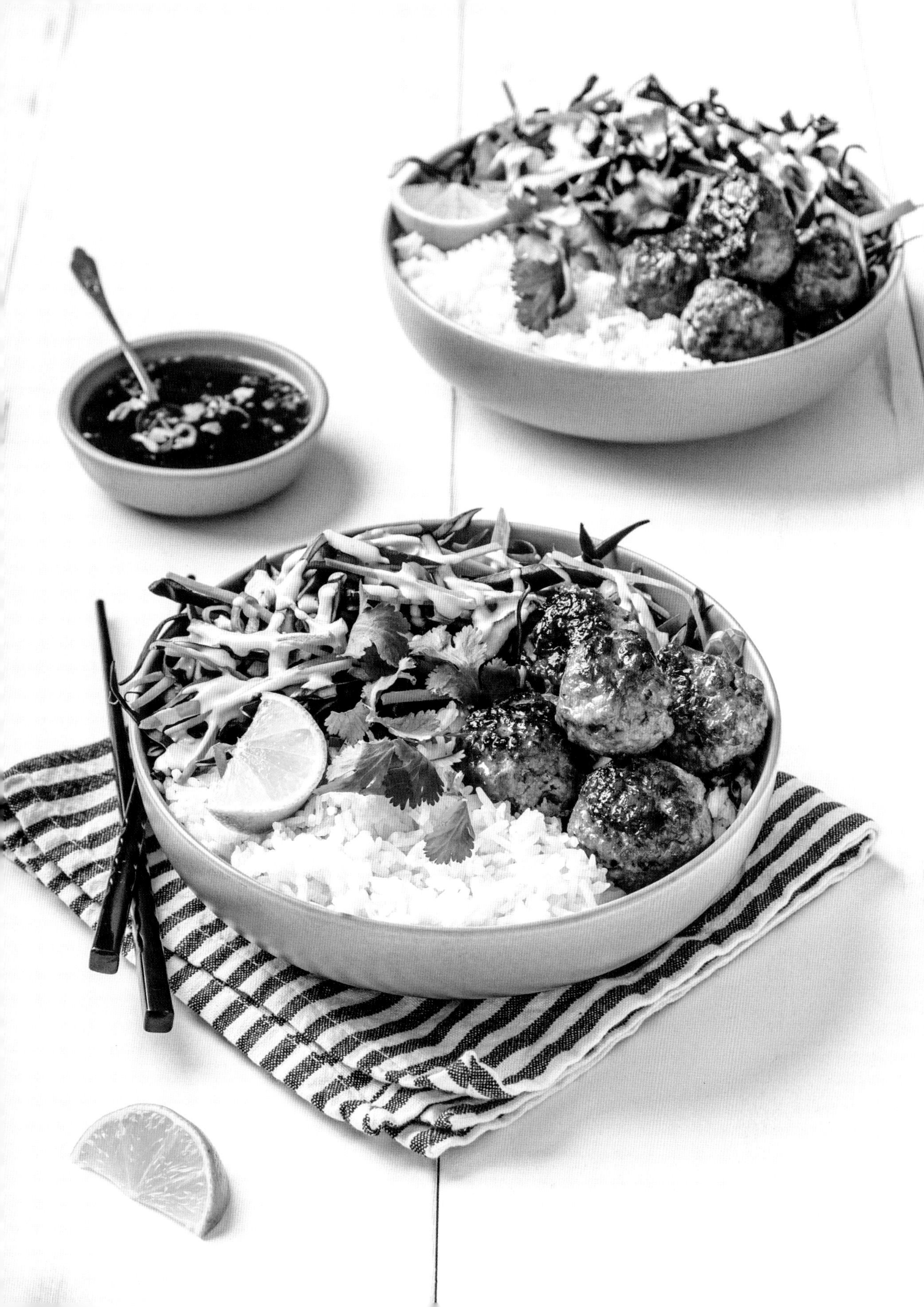

Asian Slaw

A spicy twist on a classic

Dressing

¼ cup (75 g) mayonnaise
2 teaspoons lime juice
½ teaspoon sriracha
½ teaspoon fish sauce
1 teaspoon caster sugar
1 small clove garlic, crushed

Slaw

1 large carrot, grated or cut into
    matchsticks
3 cups (240 g) finely shredded
    red cabbage
2 tablespoons finely chopped
    coriander leaves
2 green onions (dark part), finely sliced

STEPS

1. To make the **dressing**, mix all the ingredients together in a bowl.
Taste and add more sugar or sriracha if you feel it needs more sweetness or
heat. Add more mayonnaise if it is too spicy.

2. Combine the **slaw** ingredients in a large bowl. Drizzle dressing over slaw
and toss to coat.

NOTES

Dietary: For vegans, substitute a vegan
fish sauce or light soy sauce for the fish
sauce.

Substitutions: If you're short on time, use
a 250 g bag of pre-made slaw instead
of making it from scratch.

Zingy Chicken Tray Bake

Lime + coriander + Mexican spice mix = flavour bomb!

SERVES 4
PREP 15 minutes + marinating time
COOK 45 minutes

4 large skin-on, bone-in chicken
    thigh cutlets
500 g potato, peeled or unpeeled,
    cubed
500 g sweet potato, peeled and sliced
    into rounds
2 carrots, sliced
1 red onion, cut into wedges
1 tablespoon olive oil
¼ cup (60 ml) chicken stock
1 red capsicum, sliced

Marinade
¼ cup coriander leaves, finely chopped
finely grated zest and juice of 1 lime
3–4 cloves garlic, crushed
2 tablespoons olive oil
1 tablespoon brown sugar

Spice mix
1 teaspoon ground cumin
1 teaspoon paprika
1 teaspoon salt
1 teaspoon garlic powder
½ teaspoon ground black pepper
¼ teaspoon cayenne pepper

To serve
coriander leaves

PREP

✓ To make the **marinade**, mix the coriander, lime zest and juice, garlic, oil and sugar in a large bowl or container.

✓ For the **spice mix**, combine the ingredients in a small bowl. Measure a tablespoon then store the remainder in an airtight container until ready to cook.

✓ Stir 1 tablespoon of the spice mix into the marinade. Add the chicken to the bowl with the marinade and turn to coat well on all sides. Cover and marinate in the fridge for 1 hour or up to 24 hours.

✓ When ready to cook, preheat the oven to 200°C and remove the marinated chicken from the fridge.

COOK

1. Place the potato, sweet potato, carrot and onion into your largest rimmed baking tray or baking dish. Sprinkle the remaining spice mix over the veggies, drizzle with the oil and toss to coat well. Pour the chicken stock into the corner of the tray so that it doesn't wash off the seasoning.

2. Add the marinated chicken to the dish and place on a rack in the bottom third of the oven. Bake for 45 minutes or until chicken is cooked through. Add in the capsicum after 20 minutes.

3. To serve, divide between plates, drizzle with pan juices and sprinkle with fresh coriander.

NOTES

Coriander: If you don't like coriander, you can make this dish without it, just reduce the brown sugar to 2 teaspoons.

Leftovers: Store in the fridge for up to 2 days or the freezer for up to 1 month. Reheat in the microwave, or in the oven in a foil-covered ovenproof dish.

Substitutions: Substitute chicken drumsticks or marylands for the thigh cutlets, with the same cooking time. You can also marinate boneless chicken thighs, breast or tenderloins and add them in for the final 20 minutes of baking.

Vegetables: When corn is in season, you can add sliced corn cobs into the tray bake. Zucchini also works well in this dish. Both vegetables can be added in for the final 20–25 minutes.

Meatball Bánh Mì

The pickled veg is everything

16–20 leftover cooked Vietnamese
　　Meatballs (page 42)
4 Vietnamese bread rolls, halved
　　lengthways

Speedy pickled vegetables
2 tablespoons rice wine vinegar
2 tablespoons caster sugar
½ teaspoon salt
1 large (or 2 small) carrot, coarsely
　　grated or cut into matchsticks
½ continental cucumber, thinly sliced

Sriracha mayo
¼ cup (75 g) mayonnaise
2 teaspoons sriracha, or to taste

To serve
coriander leaves

STEPS

1. To make the **speedy pickled vegetables**, mix the rice wine vinegar, 1 tablespoon water, sugar and salt together in a medium bowl. Add the carrot and cucumber, toss to combine and set aside.

2. For the **sriracha mayo**, mix the mayonnaise and sriracha in a small bowl. Taste and adjust to your desired level of heat.

3. Reheat the **Vietnamese Meatballs** in the microwave, oven or air fryer.

4. Spread the sriracha mayo on the inside of the bread rolls (both sides). Drain the pickled vegetables.

5. Add meatballs to the rolls with a generous amount of pickled vegetables and garnish with fresh coriander leaves.

NOTES

Additions: I'll often add a few drops of Maggi Seasoning into the sriracha mayo and top them with fresh chilli for a more authentic flavour. If you can get your hands on a daikon radish, it can be pickled with the carrot and cucumber.

Bread: Vietnamese bread rolls are crusty on the outside and soft on the inside. They can be purchased from some supermarkets or at any good Vietnamese bakery. The best substitute would be a baguette cut into smaller pieces or any crusty long bread roll.

Leftovers: Wrap them up and pop them in lunchboxes the next day!

Pickled vegetables: These can be made ahead and kept in their liquid in a jar or container in the fridge for up to one week.

Buttermilk Fried Chicken

Juicy chicken strips coated in crispy perfection

SERVES 4
PREP 15 minutes + marinating time
COOK 20 minutes

800 g chicken tenderloins or
    breast fillet
vegetable oil, to fry

Buttermilk marinade
1 cup (250 ml) milk
1 tablespoon white vinegar
2 teaspoons salt
½ teaspoon paprika
½ teaspoon cayenne pepper

Coating
2 cups (300 g) plain flour
2 teaspoons baking powder
1 teaspoon salt
1 teaspoon paprika
1 teaspoon garlic powder
¾ teaspoon ground black pepper
½ teaspoon cayenne pepper
5 tablespoons buttermilk marinade

To serve
steamed greens
Creamy Mash (page 52)
Fried Chicken Gravy (page 53)

PREP

- ✓ To make the **buttermilk marinade**, combine the milk and vinegar in a shallow bowl or container. Stir and set aside for 5 minutes to separate (curdle). Add the salt, paprika and cayenne pepper and stir together.

- ✓ If using breast fillet, cut into tenderloin-sized strips. Add chicken to the marinade, cover and refrigerate for 1 hour or up to 24 hours.

COOK

1. Remove the chicken from the fridge.

2. For the **coating**, mix the flour, baking powder, salt, paprika, garlic powder, black pepper and cayenne pepper together in a shallow bowl. Remove chicken from fridge and add 5 tablespoons of the marinade sauce to the coating mixture, stirring loosely together until even clumps of the dry mix are spread throughout.

3. Working in batches, place the chicken into the coating mixture and turn to coat well on both sides. Transfer to a plate or tray.

4. Pour at least 5 cm of oil into a large deep pan or wok. Heat over high heat until hot, then reduce heat to medium-high.

5. Fry the chicken a few pieces at a time for around 8 minutes, turning with tongs once the bottom side is golden brown. Transfer to a plate lined with paper towel or a wire rack.

6. Serve with steamed green beans, **Creamy Mash** and **Fried Chicken Gravy** (or sides of your choice).

NOTES

Buttermilk: The milk and vinegar combination is a homemade version of buttermilk. This can be used in cakes, pancakes or any recipe that calls for buttermilk.

Frying: You can use a deep fryer but you'll use a lot more oil. I prefer to shallow fry in a pot or large wok and top up the oil if necessary. I aim to maintain a temperature of around 170°C. Any flavourless oil that's suitable for frying can be used. You can also strain and funnel your oil into a jar or bottle and reuse next time you're frying chicken.

Leftovers: Store-cooked chicken in the fridge for up to 2 days. Reheat in the oven or air fryer, or serve cold for lunches on wraps or sliced in salads. Uncooked chicken can be frozen for up to 1 month in the marinade, then coated and fried once defrosted.

Creamy Mash

Pillowy mouthfuls of potato

SERVES 4
PREP 10 minutes
COOK 25 minutes

1 kg potatoes, peeled and cut into
   3–4 cm cubes
2 tablespoons + 1 teaspoon salt
3 tablespoons unsalted butter, cubed,
   at room temperature
⅓ cup (80 ml) room-temperature milk

PREP

- ✓ Peel potatoes and cut into 3–4 cm cubes.
- ✓ Put a large pot of salted water on to boil.

COOK

1. Add the potatoes to the water and turn the heat up to high. Ensure that the water is at least 3 cm above the top of the potatoes. Once the water is boiling, reduce the heat to medium-low and simmer, uncovered, for 12–15 minutes or until the potatoes are tender.

2. Drain the potatoes well in a colander then transfer them back into the empty pot on the stovetop with the heat on low. Gently move the potatoes around in the pot for 30–60 seconds so that most of the moisture and steam can evaporate, then remove the pot from the heat.

3. Mash the potatoes in the pot with a masher until smooth, then add the butter and 1 teaspoon salt. Mash again until well combined. Pour in about half of the milk then slowly keep adding more, until you reach your preferred consistency.

4. Give it a good stir with a large spoon, taste and season with pepper and more salt if you wish, then serve immediately.

NOTES

Leftovers: Store in the fridge for up to 4 days. Use leftovers to make potato pancakes or fried mashed potato balls.

Level up: Using warmed or room temperature dairy in your mash will help it to be as soft and fluffy as possible. Cold dairy will cool down your mash and can cause the texture to become gluey.

Potatoes: For the creamiest mash, it's best to choose a potato that's labelled as suitable for mashing. I recommend: Dutch cream, sebago, desiree, coliban and nicola.

Fried Chicken Gravy

Also delish over mash, just like the KFC version

2 chicken stock cubes
1 beef stock cube
1¾ cups (430 ml) boiling water
3 tablespoons unsalted butter
3 tablespoons plain flour
¼ teaspoon garlic powder
¼ teaspoon ground black or
  white pepper

PREP

✓ Crumble the chicken and beef stock cubes into a heatproof jug. Add the boiling water and stir to dissolve. Set aside.

COOK

1. Heat the butter in a small saucepan over medium-low heat until melted.

2. Add the flour to the pan with the garlic powder and pepper. Stir the flour and butter together to make a paste (roux) and continue stirring until it begins to brown.

3. Pour the stock in slowly while stirring or whisking continuously. Raise the heat to medium and bring the gravy to a simmer. Keep stirring for a couple of minutes or until the gravy thickens.

4. Taste and season with salt and pepper.

NOTES

Credit: I found a KFC gravy copycat recipe many years ago on an obscure food blog called *Best of Ready to Cook*. I've since adapted the recipe and it has evolved into this one.

Leftovers: Store in the fridge for up to 4 days. Freeze for up to 3 months. Reheat on the stovetop, adding a little extra stock if needed.

Vegetable Massaman Curry

A mild, veg-packed Thai favourite

1 brown onion, thinly sliced or diced
4 cloves garlic, crushed
1 tablespoon finely grated fresh ginger
500 g sweet potato, peeled and cubed
500 g potatoes, peeled and cubed
4 carrots, sliced
300 g green beans, trimmed and
    halved
1 red capsicum, thinly sliced
1 tablespoon vegetable oil
2 × 114 g tins massaman curry paste
3 × 400 g tins coconut cream
1 tablespoon lime juice (about ½ lime)
1 tablespoon brown sugar
1 tablespoon fish sauce

To serve
steamed jasmine or basmati rice
lime wedges
coriander leaves

PREP

✓ Slice onion, crush garlic and grate ginger.

✓ Peel potatoes, sweet potatoes and carrots. Chop potatoes into 2cm cubes, sweet potatoes into 3cm cubes and carrots into 1cm slices.

✓ Trim and halve green beans and slice capsicum.

COOK

1. Heat the oil in a large frying pan or pot over medium-high heat. Add the onion and cook, stirring, for 2 minutes. Add the curry paste, garlic and ginger. Cook, stirring, for 2 minutes.

2. Pour in ½ tin of coconut cream and cook, stirring, for 2–3 minutes, until the liquid has visibly reduced by about a third. Pour in the remaining coconut cream then add lime juice, brown sugar and fish sauce. Bring to the boil.

3. Add the sweet potato, potato and carrot then reduce heat to medium-low. Simmer, partially covered, for about 15 minutes or until the vegetables are tender. Add the beans and capsicum and cook for another 5 minutes or until vegetables are cooked to your liking.

4. Taste to check spice level and flavour. Add a little more lime juice, sugar or fish sauce if you feel that it needs acidity, sweetness or salt.

5. Serve over rice, with lime wedges on the side and topped with coriander leaves.

NOTES

Curry paste: I like to use Maesri brand of curry paste. I use a ratio of 2 tins curry paste to 3 tins coconut cream for a mild-medium curry. For a very mild curry, use 1 tin curry paste.

Dietary: For vegans, substitute a vegan fish sauce or light soy sauce for the fish sauce.

Leftovers: Store in the fridge for up to 3 days or the freezer for up to 3 months. Reheat in the microwave or on the stovetop.

Meat: 400 g (or more) cubed or sliced raw chicken breast can be added to the curry at step 3. Reduce the amount of potato and sweet potato you use if adding chicken.

Spice level: If the curry is too spicy, add a little vegetable or chicken stock. You could also add more coconut cream if you have some.

Vegetables: The hard veggies such as potato and carrot should be cut into 1 cm cubes or they will take much longer to cook.

Pork Noodle Stir-Fry

In my home we call these 'food-court noodles' – they're SO good!

2 cups reserved (and defrosted)
  Vietnamese Meatball mixture
  (page 42)
2 carrots, thinly sliced
200 g green beans, trimmed and
  cut into thirds
3 cups (240 g) finely shredded
  red cabbage
2 green onions, sliced (keep pale and
  dark parts separate)
800 g shelf-fresh hokkien noodles
2 tablespoons vegetable oil
sriracha (optional)

Sauce
1 tablespoon cornflour
2 tablespoons water or chicken stock
3 tablespoons dark soy sauce
3 tablespoons light soy sauce
3 tablespoons oyster sauce

PREP

✓ Remove the **Vietnamese Meatball** mixture from the fridge and set aside
  on the bench.

✓ Peel and slice the carrot, chop green beans, shred cabbage and slice the
  green onions, separating the dark green from the white/light green slices.

✓ Prepare the noodles according to packet instructions.

✓ To make the **sauce**, place cornflour into a bowl and gradually add the
  water or chicken stock, stirring until smooth. Stir in the remaining
  ingredients. Set aside.

COOK

1. Heat half the oil in a wok or large frying pan over high heat. Add the
meatball mixture to the pan. Spread it out and let it caramelise on one side for
a couple of minutes before breaking it up. Cook until well browned. Remove
from pan and transfer to a plate.

2. Heat the remaining oil in the pan and add the carrot and pale part of the
green onion. Stir-fry for a minute or two then add the beans and cabbage and
stir-fry for another minute.

3. Give the sauce a quick whisk then pour it into the pan. Stir through for
30 seconds then add the noodles and cooked meatball mixture. Stir-fry for a
couple of minutes, until well coated in the thick glossy sauce. Taste and add
a dash of sriracha if you'd like some heat.

4. Divide between serving bowls and sprinkle with the dark green onions.

NOTES

Leftovers: Store in the fridge for up to
2 days. Reheat in the microwave or on
the stovetop.

Noodles: You could substitute the
hokkien noodles with any egg noodles
or rice noodles. Be very gentle when
separating and preparing fresh noodles
as they break easily. If you purchase
400 g packs as I do, you'll need two for
this recipe.

Vegetables: Any stir-fry vegetables
can be used for this dish, either frozen
or fresh.

Comfort
Food

Week 3

Sunday

Italian Spaghetti Meatballs

Monday

Vegetable Frittata

Tuesday

Meatball Subs

Wednesday

Pan-Fried Fish with
Smashed Potatoes

Thursday

Italian Wedding Soup

Friday

Chicken Fried Rice

Saturday

Veggie Mac 'n' Cheese

Week 3 at a Glance

 **28 meals**
plus 8 leftovers

 **$2.39**
per serving

I make no apologies for this one week of dairy and carb-loaded recipes! For those with dietary restrictions, you may be tempted to skip over this plan, but first, please take a look at some of the simple substitutions in the recipe notes to convert them to gluten-free and dairy-free meals.

Sunday

We start the week by batch cooking three meals worth of Italian Spaghetti Meatballs. A third of the mixture will be rolled into small meatballs, cooked today and frozen for the Italian Wedding Soup. The remaining two-thirds will be rolled into 30–35 medium-sized meatballs and divided between tonight's Spaghetti Meatballs and Tuesday's Meatball Subs (pop 16 meatballs with about 2 cups of the remaining sauce in the fridge for these). Depending on your family's appetite you may have leftover medium meatballs and sauce. Save them to make additional Meatball Subs or freeze the meatballs in the sauce for up to three months.

Monday

This Vegetable Frittata is a simple but tasty weeknight meal taking just 40 minutes to prep and cook. Leftovers can be eaten cold or reheated for lunch and the combinations for fillings are endless. It's gluten-free and a fabulous option for a weekend brunch or lunch. Use half the bag of baby spinach in tonight's recipe and save the other half for the Italian Wedding Soup.

Tuesday

You'll have dinner on the table tonight in about 20 minutes flat. My 'secret sauce' for these Meatball Subs is the garlic butter. It adds an extra layer of flavour and, come on, who doesn't love garlic butter?! If you have 2 bread rolls remaining, save them to serve with Thursday's soup.

Wednesday

There are a few components to tonight's dinner – the Pan-Fried Fish, the lemon garlic butter sauce, the Smashed Potatoes and the steamed green beans. As always, I recommend that you read the recipes through a couple of times before getting started. Each element is very simple, you just need to get the timing right – but don't worry, I've left directions for you in the recipe notes! I've allocated 250 g of beans in the shopping list for tonight's dinner but it's up to you if you'd like to swap them out for a salad or some steamed broccolini.

Thursday

Tonight's Italian Wedding Soup is one of my favourites, which is why you're making a double batch. I'm confident that you'll enjoy it as much as I do and will be very pleased to have leftovers in the fridge or in the freezer for a rainy day. This recipe can be made in under 30 minutes. If you have an appetite for even more carbs, serve the soup with some warm crusty bread or garlic bread made from your leftover bread rolls.

Friday

It's Fakeaway Friday again and we're making a very simple Chicken Fried Rice. This is also your opportunity to use up any remnants of stir-fry-suitable veggies in the fridge or freezer. If you have the time, make your rice earlier in the day or the night before.

Saturday

I truly believe that this Veggie Mac 'n' Cheese is far superior to the 'mac-only' version. It's also a great dish for entertaining because you can make it ahead, pop it in the fridge and bake it in the oven when your guests arrive. If you'd like to add some meaty flavour, chopped ham or bacon work a treat.

Week 3 Grocery List

Ingredients in italics are Pantry Staples (page 11), so you may have them already.

Meat and Fish

- 1 kg beef mince
- 500 g pork mince
- 600–800 g fresh or thawed white fish fillets
- 200–300 g chicken breast fillet

Fruit and Veg

- 1 kg baby red or white potatoes
- 1 bunch green onions
- 280 g bag baby spinach
- 3 brown onions
- 3 bulbs garlic
- 4 large carrots
- 2 heads broccoli (about 400–500 g)
- 350 g green beans
- ½ cauliflower (about 350 g)
- 1 large bunch flat-leaf parsley
- 1 red capsicum
- 1 lemon

Fridge and Freezer

- 500 g extra tasty cheese
- *unsalted butter*
- *17 eggs*
- 1.2 litres *full cream milk*
- *parmesan*

Pantry

- 2 × 700 g bottles passata
- 6 pack long crusty bread rolls
- 500 g macaroni
- 500 g spaghetti or fettuccine
- *olive oil*
- *vegetable oil*
- *salt*
- *pepper*
- *paprika*
- *dried oregano*
- *cayenne pepper*
- *dried chilli flakes*
- *garlic powder*
- *caster sugar*
- *jasmine rice*
- *plain flour*
- *sesame oil*
- *light soy sauce*
- *oyster sauce*
- *beef stock cubes/powder*
- *chicken stock cubes/powder*
- *panko breadcrumbs*

Week 3 Swap 'n' Save

Some weeks the budget is tighter than others, or you're more busy, more tired, have unexpected guests, want to mix things up, or are catering for dietary preferences. Use the tips below to make adjustments to suit.

⊙ Swap out

chicken breast ⟶ chicken thigh or chicken mince

baby spinach ⟶ frozen spinach, silverbeet or kale

red capsicum ⟶ green capsicum

passata ⟶ crushed tomatoes

extra tasty cheese ⟶ colby, cheddar or any melting cheese

bunch of green onions ⟶ 1 additional large brown onion

jasmine rice ⟶ long grain rice

ⓢ Pocket some savings

Passata: Buy the cheapest passata you can find. Plain tomato is fine, as you'll be adding plenty of flavour into the meatball sauce with additional seasonings.

Shop seasonally: Choose seasonal vegetables to replace the broccoli, green beans and capsicum if prices for these are too high.

Ugly produce: The cost of a 1 kg bag of carrots (particularly the 'ugly' ones) will most likely be cheaper than buying 4 individual carrots.

Fish: The major supermarkets often run specials on the thawed barramundi product they sell at the seafood counter (from 30–50 per cent off), making it affordable for most. This is my top pick for the Pan-Fried Fish recipe. However, any white fish can be used. The ideal fillet is one that is less than 3 cm thick and reasonably firm.

Shortcut

If you're short on time this week, for the 3 meatball-based recipes in this plan you have the option of buying pre-made meatballs from your butcher or the supermarket. You'll need about 1.5 kg worth of meatballs (usually 3 packs). They won't be as flavour-filled as my Italian Meatballs but you'll still make 3 very tasty meals!

⊙ Leftovers

If you cook all the recipes as written, you shouldn't have any leftover ingredients, aside from your pantry staples.

Italian Spaghetti Meatballs

Guaranteed to melt in your mouth!

SERVES 12
PREP 20 minutes
COOK 30 minutes

3 eggs
¾ cup (55 g) panko breadcrumbs
¾ cup (180 ml) milk
¾ cup (60 g) grated or shaved
   parmesan
6–8 cloves garlic, crushed
1 tablespoon salt
1½ teaspoons ground black pepper
1 teaspoon dried chilli flakes
1 tablespoon dried oregano or dried
   Italian herbs
⅔ cup flat-leaf parsley leaves,
   finely chopped
1 kg beef mince
500 g pork mince
2–4 tablespoons olive oil, for frying

To serve
500 g spaghetti, cooked
Italian Meatball Sauce (page 67)
finely grated or shaved parmesan
finely chopped flat-leaf parsley leaves

NOTES

Gluten-free: Use grated gluten-free bread or breadcrumbs. Serve meatballs over mashed potatoes.

Leftovers: The meatballs can be frozen (raw or cooked) for up to 3 months. Store in the fridge for up to 3 days and reheat in the microwave.

Make ahead: I prefer to make these at least an hour ahead as refrigerating helps them set.

Meal plan: If cooking as part of the meal plan, reserve 16 meatballs in sauce for the Meatball Subs.

Mince: Any combination of beef, veal or pork mince will work for this recipe, ideally at least 50 per cent beef. You can use a fattier mince for these: 10–20 per cent fat works well.

PREP

✓ Beat the eggs in the largest mixing bowl you have. Add the breadcrumbs and milk and stir together well. Set aside for 5 minutes to soften.

✓ Add parmesan, garlic, salt, pepper, chilli, oregano and parsley to the egg mixture and stir well to combine. Add the beef and pork mince and use your hands to gently combine the ingredients together. You want to ensure that you're not overmixing it.

✓ For this week's meal plan, separate the mixture into two portions: one-third to make small meatballs, and two-thirds to make medium-sized meatballs.

✓ To make the medium balls, roll 1½ tablespoons mixture for each ball. To make the smaller balls, roll ½ tablespoon mixture for each ball. All the meatballs will be cooked tonight, to get ahead for the week.

COOK

1. If you're planning on serving these meatballs with spaghetti tonight according to the meal plan, then you'll need enough cooked spaghetti for four people. Pop this on to cook while the meatballs simmer.

2. Heat 2 tablespoons of the oil in a large frying pan over medium-high heat. Cook the medium-sized meatballs in batches until just browned on all sides. Set aside.

3. Heat the remaining oil if necessary. Cook the small meatballs for 4–5 minutes, until cooked through. Transfer to a plate or tray lined with paper towel to drain and set aside to cool. Place the cooled small meatballs in an airtight container and freeze. Remove to defrost overnight, the day before using them for the Italian Wedding Soup.

4. Meanwhile, gently place the medium-sized meatballs in the simmering Italian Meatball Sauce. Cook on low heat, partially covered, for at least 20 minutes or until cooked through. Depending on your family's appetite you'll use about half of these in tonight's Italian Spaghetti Meatballs (serves 4). Pop the leftover meatballs and sauce in the fridge for Tuesday night's Meatball Subs.

SERVE

For tonight's Italian Spaghetti Meatballs, spoon about half the meatball and sauce mixture over cooked spaghetti. Sprinkle with parmesan and parsley.

Italian Meatball Sauce

A simple, rich napoletana sauce

1 brown onion, very finely diced
6 large cloves garlic, crushed
2 tablespoons olive oil
1 tablespoon dried oregano or mixed Italian herbs
2 teaspoons salt
1 teaspoon dried chilli flakes
2 × 700 g bottles passata
pinch caster sugar (optional)

PREP

✓ Finely dice the brown onion and crush the garlic cloves.

COOK

1. Heat the oil in a large frying pan or saucepan over medium heat. Add the onion and cook, stirring, for a few minutes or until translucent. Add garlic and cook for 1 minute, then add oregano, salt, chilli and passata.

2. Increase heat to medium-high and bring the sauce to a gentle boil. Turn it down to low and simmer for at least 10 minutes. Taste and add more oregano, chilli or salt if necessary. If the sauce tastes acidic, add the pinch of sugar.

3. Keep hot to cook the meatballs or reheat when ready to use.

WEEK 3

NOTES

Flavour boost: Add 2 tablespoons tomato paste and ¼ cup (60 ml) red wine before the passata. Let it cook off for a few minutes before adding the passata.

Leftovers: Any leftover sauce can be frozen for up to 6 months or stored in the fridge for up to 4 days.

Pasta sauce: This is a quick tasty sauce that can be halved or doubled and holds its own as a standalone recipe, coating any pasta shape.

Timing: From start to finish, the sauce, meatballs and pasta should take about 60–70 minutes. Start the sauce prior to cooking the meatballs so they can be added to the sauce once seared. Cook the spaghetti while the meatballs are cooking in the sauce.

Vegetable Frittata

Serve it up for breakfast, lunch or dinner

SERVES 4–5
PREP 15 minutes
COOK 30 minutes

1 cup (100 g) grated extra tasty cheese
2 tablespoons finely grated parmesan
½ brown onion, diced
½ red capsicum, diced
2 cloves garlic, crushed
1 head broccoli (400–500 g),
    broken up into small florets
2 green onions, pale parts finely diced,
    dark part thinly sliced
10 eggs
¼ cup (60 ml) milk
1 tablespoon olive oil
140 g baby spinach

PREP

✓ Preheat the oven to 180°C.

✓ Grate the cheeses, dice the onion and capsicum. Crush the garlic and chop the broccoli into small florets. Finely dice the pale parts of the green onion and thinly slice the dark green part.

✓ Crack the eggs into a medium bowl, add milk and whisk together. Stir in about ¾ of the tasty cheese and parmesan. Season well with salt and pepper.

COOK

1. Heat the oil in a large non-stick, ovenproof frying pan or cast iron pan over medium heat. Add the brown onion to the pan and cook, stirring, for a couple of minutes. Add the diced green onion, broccoli, capsicum and garlic and cook for another few minutes, until just tender. Add the baby spinach and stir until wilted.

2. Spread the vegetables out evenly in the pan then pour the egg mixture over the top. Sprinkle with the remaining cheese. Cook without stirring for 2–3 minutes or until the egg at the outside edge starts to set.

3. Carefully transfer the pan onto a rack in the middle of the oven. Bake for 17–20 minutes, or until fully set.

4. Allow to rest in the pan for a few minutes then slide out onto a plate. Slice into wedges and serve sprinkled with sliced green onion.

NOTES

Flavour boost: Chorizo, ham or bacon add extra flavour, but you can also experiment with spices – try 1 teaspoon of paprika or dried chilli flakes. If you have excess parsley, finely chop and sprinkle 1 or 2 tablespoons over the top before baking.

Leftovers: Store in the fridge for up to 3 days or the freezer for up to 3 months. Reheat in the microwave, or in the oven in a foil-covered ovenproof dish. It can also be served cold for lunch.

Substitutions: Frozen spinach can be used in place of baby spinach. Thaw and squeeze out as much excess liquid as possible.

Vegetables: You can use any combination of vegetables for this frittata. Just maintain the same approximate ratios: 10 eggs, ¼ cup milk, 1 cup grated cheese, 3–4 cups chopped veggies.

Meatball Subs

Satisfying Italian–American classic

16 leftover medium Italian Spaghetti
    Meatballs (page 64) with Italian
    Meatball Sauce (page 67)
4 long crusty bread rolls
1 cup (100 g) grated extra tasty cheese

Simple garlic butter
45 g unsalted butter, softened
1 clove garlic, crushed
¼ teaspoon salt

To serve
parsley leaves

PREP

✓ Preheat the oven to 200°C on the grill setting. Line a baking tray with foil.

✓ To make the simple garlic butter, mix the ingredients together in a small bowl.

✓ Heat the meatballs and sauce in the microwave or on the stovetop. Meanwhile, halve the bread rolls lengthways so they are still attached on one side.

COOK

1. Spread a thin layer of garlic butter over both sides of the bread rolls. Place them butter-side up on the baking tray and heat under the grill for a couple of minutes.

2. Remove the tray from the oven. Place 4 meatballs on each roll with your desired amount of sauce and top with grated cheese. Put back under the grill and cook until the cheese is melted and starts to brown. Remove, sprinkle with parsley leaves and serve immediately.

NOTES

Flavour boost: For some contrasting colour and flavour, add fresh basil or rocket leaves.

Sides: This can be served as is, for a light weeknight meal or weekend lunch. You can bulk it up by serving with fries and/or a green salad.

Pan-Fried Fish with Lemon Garlic Butter Sauce

Resist the temptation to drink the sauce!

SERVES 4
PREP 10 minutes
COOK 20 minutes

600–800 g white fish fillets
1 tablespoon olive oil
3 tablespoons unsalted butter
1 large clove garlic, crushed
juice of ½ lemon

To serve
1 tablespoon finely chopped flat-leaf
    parsley leaves
steamed green beans
lemon wedges
Smashed Potatoes (page 75)

PREP

✓ Cut fillets into smaller pieces if necessary. Pat dry with a paper towel. Try to remove as much excess moisture as possible, particularly if they have been frozen and thawed.

COOK

1. Heat a large frying pan or cast iron pan over medium-high heat then add the oil. Place half the fillets into the pan and cook for about 4 minutes on one side without disturbing. Carefully turn over with a spatula and cook the other side for 4 minutes or until lightly browned and cooked through. Place the cooked fish on a plate and tent it with foil to keep warm while you fry the remaining fillets.

2. Once all the fish is cooked, turn the heat down on the stove to the lowest setting. Add the butter to the pan and then the garlic. Cook for 1–2 minutes, until soft. If it looks like it's browning quickly, move it off the heat. Add the lemon juice and stir it into the garlic butter.

3. Divide the fish and Smashed Potatoes between plates. Spoon the sauce over the fish, and any excess over the smashed potatoes. Sprinkle with parsley. Serve with steamed green beans and lemon wedges.

NOTES

Dairy-free: Skip the garlic butter sauce and squeeze fresh lemon juice over the fish, or use a dairy-free butter alternative.

Fish: Skin-off barramundi is my personal favourite but I've also cooked this with perch and basa. Any white fish can be used, just ensure that it's not too thick – ideally no more than 3 cm. I allow 150–200 g fish per person.

Sauce: If you love the idea of lots of garlic buttery lemon sauce to pour over your fish and potatoes, you can double the ingredients for the sauce.

Timing: It should take about 20 minutes to prep and cook the fish. If you're making Smashed Potatoes you can prep the fish while the potatoes are boiling. Start cooking the fish when the potatoes go into the oven. Steam 250 g trimmed green beans for 5–7 minutes just before serving.

Smashed Potatoes

Ultra crispy and addictive

1 kg baby white or red potatoes,
   skin on
2 tablespoons olive oil
1 tablespoon finely chopped
   flat-leaf parsley leaves

STEPS

1. Preheat the oven to 200°C on the grill setting. Lightly oil a large baking tray.

2. Place the potatoes into a large pot of salted water over high heat and bring to the boil. Cook for 25–30 minutes or until tender, then drain in a colander.

3. Place the potatoes on the baking tray and 'smash' by gently pressing down on them with a potato masher or the base of a large glass. Season well with salt and pepper and drizzle olive oil over each potato.

4. Place the tray under the grill and cook for 15 minutes or until the potatoes reach your desired level of crispiness. Remove from the oven, sprinkle with parsley and serve immediately.

NOTES

Flavour boost: If you're serving this with the pan-fried fish, drizzle any leftover lemon garlic butter sauce over the potatoes.

Leftovers: Store in the fridge for up to 3 days. They can be reheated in the microwave but to maintain crispiness, reheat in the oven or air fryer.

Timing: If you're following the meal plan, start prepping the fish while the potatoes are boiling and start cooking it just after you put the potatoes under the grill. Everything should be ready at the same time.

Italian Wedding Soup

Light, fresh, low-fuss

1½ brown onions, diced
3 large carrots, diced
4 cloves garlic, crushed
2 tablespoons olive oil
8 cups (2 litres) chicken stock
1 cup (250 ml) beef stock
1 cup (125 g) macaroni or other small
    pasta shape
cooked small **Italian Spaghetti
Meatballs** (page 65), thawed if frozen
140 g baby spinach leaves

To serve
finely grated parmesan
finely chopped flat-leaf parsley leaves
garlic bread or crusty bread

PREP

✓ Dice the onions and carrots and crush the garlic.

COOK

1. Heat the oil in a large saucepan or pot over medium heat. Add the onion, carrot and celery (if using) and cook for 5 minutes or until the vegetables are softened. Add garlic and cook for another minute, stirring.

2. Pour the chicken stock, beef stock and 1 cup (250 ml) water into the pot. Raise heat to medium-high to bring just to the boil, then reduce to medium again.

3. Add the pasta and cook, uncovered, for about 8 minutes. Add the meatballs and spinach and simmer for another few minutes, until heated through and pasta is tender.

4. Season with salt and pepper to taste. Serve sprinkled with parmesan and parsley and with garlic bread or crusty bread on the side.

NOTES

Dairy-free: Leave off the parmesan, and serve with crusty bread rather than garlic bread.

Leftovers: Store in the fridge for up to 3 days. The soup can be frozen for up to 3 months, if the frozen meatballs were thawed in the fridge overnight and not in the microwave or at room temperature. Reheat in the microwave or on the stovetop.

Shortcut: Purchase pre-rolled meatballs from the butcher or supermarket. Cook them in a frying pan or bake in the oven, then add to the soup as directed.

Substitutions: Kale or silverbeet work well in place of the baby spinach. Any small pasta shape can be used, such as small shells, ditalini, risoni or even pearl couscous. If using risoni, ensure that you stir regularly to prevent the pasta sticking to the bottom of the pot.

Chicken Fried Rice

Worthy of main meal status

SERVES 5–6
PREP 15 minutes
COOK 15 minutes (using pre-cooked rice)

2 cups (200 g) jasmine rice, cooked
  and cooled (see Notes)
200–300 g chicken breast fillet,
  cut into 1–2 cm cubes
1 teaspoon light soy sauce
1½ tablespoons vegetable oil
4 eggs
3–4 green onions, pale parts finely
  chopped, dark green parts sliced
3 cloves garlic, crushed
1 large carrot, diced
½ red capsicum, diced
100 g green beans
½ head broccoli (250 g),
  chopped into small pieces
¼ cup (60 ml) light soy sauce,
  extra, plus more to taste
1½ tablespoons oyster sauce
2 teaspoons sesame oil

PREP

✓ If using freshly cooked rice, spread it out on a large tray or plate and pop it in the fridge, uncovered, for at least a few minutes to allow some of the moisture to evaporate.

✓ Combine the chicken, soy sauce and 1 teaspoon of the vegetable oil in a bowl. Set aside.

✓ Beat the eggs in a small bowl and season with salt and pepper.

✓ Finely chop the pale parts of the green onions and slice the dark green parts. Crush the garlic, peel and dice the carrot, dice the capsicum, trim and chop the green beans, chop the broccoli into small pieces.

COOK

1. Heat 1 teaspoon oil in a wok or your largest frying pan over medium-high heat. Add the egg, cooking and stirring until scrambled. Transfer to a bowl and wipe out the wok.

2. Turn the heat up to high, add 2 teaspoons oil and stir-fry the chicken for 3–4 minutes, until lightly browned and cooked through. Transfer to the bowl with the eggs.

3. Heat another 2 teaspoons oil in the wok. Stir-fry the finely chopped green onion and garlic for a minute then add the rest of the veggies. Stir-fry for a couple of minutes, until just tender.

4. Add the rice, sauces and sesame oil to the wok and stir-fry for a few minutes, then add the egg and chicken. Stir through until evenly combined.

5. Taste and add more soy sauce if you want to amp up the flavour (but be careful it doesn't get too salty!).

6. Garnish with sliced green onions then serve immediately.

NOTES

Flavour boost: I like to add a few drops of Maggi seasoning in the last minute of cooking for that 'Chinese takeaway' flavour. You can also add chilli paste or sriracha sauce for a spicy kick.

Gluten-free: Use gluten-free soy sauce and oyster sauce.

Leftovers: Store in the fridge as soon as possible after cooking, for up to 2 days. Reheat in a wok or pan with 1 tablespoon oil for best results and

ensure that it is piping hot before serving. I don't recommend freezing fried rice.

Meat: Chicken thigh or chicken mince can be used in place of breast, or any alternative protein such as beef, pork or tofu. You could also add 100 g of chopped bacon.

Rice: Any long-grain rice can be used. Ideally you would pre-cook and chill the rice the day before, but if using

freshly cooked rice, spread it out on a large tray or plate and pop it in the fridge, uncovered, for at least a few minutes to allow some of the moisture to evaporate.

Vegetables: Use any suitable stir-fry vegetables, fresh or frozen. Aim for about 3 cups of chopped vegetables. 1 small diced brown onion can be used in place of the green onions.

Veggie Mac 'n' Cheese

An upgrade from the kid-friendly classic

3 cups (300 g) grated tasty cheese
½ cup (40 g) finely grated parmesan
60 g unsalted butter
5 tablespoons plain flour
3 ½ cups (875 ml) milk
½ head cauliflower (350 g) chopped
   into bite-sized florets
½ head broccoli (250 g) chopped into
   bite-sized florets
3 green onions, (pale and dark parts)
   finely sliced (optional)
3 cups (375 g) macaroni
½ teaspoon salt
½ teaspoon garlic powder

Breadcrumb topping

1 cup (75 g) panko breadcrumbs
30 g unsalted butter, melted
1 small clove garlic, crushed
½ teaspoon salt
¼ teaspoon paprika
pinch of cayenne pepper

PREP

✓ Grate cheeses, measure out butter, flour and milk and set aside.

✓ Chop cauliflower and broccoli, and slice green onions.

✓ For the breadcrumb topping, combine all the ingredients in a bowl and set aside.

COOK

1. Preheat the oven to 180°C. Bring a large pot of salted water to the boil over high heat.

2. Melt the butter in a medium saucepan over medium heat. Add the flour and cook, stirring continuously, for 1–2 minutes until bubbling.

3. Add 1 cup (250 ml) milk and stir well until the flour and butter are incorporated and there aren't any lumps. Gradually stir in the remaining milk. Cook for 8–10 minutes, stirring regularly, until thickened.

4. Turn off the heat, add the salt and garlic powder, then about ⅔ of the combined cheeses. Stir until the cheese has melted into the sauce. Taste and add more salt and/or pepper if necessary.

5. Meanwhile, cook the macaroni in the boiling water for 5 minutes. Add the cauliflower and broccoli florets and cook for another 2 minutes or until tender. You don't want either to be fully cooked because they will continue to cook in the oven later. When ready, drain in a large colander.

6. Gently tip the pasta and veggies into a large baking dish and add the green onion, if using. Pour the cheese sauce over and stir through. Spread the mixture out evenly in the dish and sprinkle with the remaining cheese. Scatter the breadcrumb topping over.

7. Bake uncovered for 15–20 minutes, or until the breadcrumb topping is light golden brown.

NOTES

Leftovers: Store in the fridge for up to 3 days or freeze for up to 2 months. Reheat in the microwave or in the oven in a covered ovenproof dish.

Make ahead: Prepare up to the end of step 6. Cover the dish with foil or cling wrap and store in the fridge for up to 24 hours. Bake uncovered for 25–30 minutes.

Pasta: Similarly sized pasta shapes such as shells, penne or farfalle can be used.

Around the World

Week 4

Sunday

Chicken Pesto Pasta

Monday

Chorizo Lentil Soup

Tuesday

Mongolian Beef

Wednesday

Chorizo Lentil Soup

Thursday

Middle Eastern Chicken
and Rice

Friday

Thai Basil Chicken Stir-Fry

Saturday

Butter Bean Stew

Week 4 at a Glance

 **28 meals**
plus 4 leftovers

 **$2.49**
per serving

This week's meals are, once again, a diverse blend of cuisines, flavours and ingredients. We're not cooking a 'base meal' this week, but we do have one night of leftovers and four recipes that can be prepped and cooked in under 30 minutes!

Sunday

If you're only going to try one recipe from this plan, this is the one! Much loved by my family and my valued group of recipe testers, the Chicken Pesto Pasta will warm your belly and satisfy those 'creamy pasta' cravings that come to call every so often. It's already packed with veg but feel free to add more! If you'd like to offset the creaminess, serve with a fresh green or garden salad. For those who aren't carb-shy, a big hunk of garlic bread marries beautifully with the sauce. This can quite easily be modified for those who are vegetarian or gluten-free.

Monday

If you're new to cooking with lentils, this Chorizo Lentil Soup is a great place to start. Red lentils don't require soaking and cook a lot quicker than their brown and green cousins. You'll use quite a few spices for this soup that create a warming, rich flavour rather than a spicy heat. Just ensure that you choose a mild chorizo if you don't like hot chilli. This should yield about 8 servings. For this meal plan, I've suggested refrigerating and serving the leftovers on Wednesday. Otherwise, freeze them for another day. Remember to marinate the beef for tomorrow night's dinner, either tonight or tomorrow morning, especially if you're using a cheaper, less tender cut of beef.

Tuesday

This Mongolian Beef is so tasty and, by far, the sauciest stir-fry that I cook. If you didn't remember to marinate the beef for at least a few hours, all is not lost! Just allow it to tenderise and marinate for at least 30 to 60 minutes prior to cooking. It may not be perfectly tender, but will still be delicious. This is quite a quick cooking dish so make sure you put the rice on before you prep the vegetables, so that everything is ready at the same time.

Wednesday

Sit back and relax because tonight all you have to do is reheat the rest of the Chorizo Lentil Soup! Serve it up with Turkish bread, grilled with a drizzle of olive oil. Remember that you can always swap 'leftover night' to another night, if it works better with your schedule this week. Because you have a bit of extra time up your sleeve, use some of it to marinate the chicken for tomorrow's dinner.

Thursday

This Middle Eastern Chicken and Rice is the most time-consuming dish of the week, but boy is it worth it! If you're tight for time tonight, swap this dish over to another night as it'll take about 1 hour 15 minutes to cook (if you've already marinated the chicken). If you forgot to marinate it, don't despair – I've made this with a 10-minute marinade – the flavour of the chicken will be slightly muted, but you'll still have a banger of a meal. While the chickpeas and spinach are optional, they do add good flavour and nutrition and help the meal go further.

Friday

For those who bypass chicken mince for the far more popular beef or pork varieties, this Thai Basil Chicken Stir-Fry will make you a fan. It's so yummy, and ready in under 30 minutes. I highly recommend topping it with the fried eggs for additional protein, colour and texture.

Saturday

This Butter Bean Stew is a light dinner that hits the spot and, as a bonus, it's dairy-free, gluten-free and vegan! I often make this for a quick weekend lunch and usually serve it accompanied by my homemade garlic bread.

Week 4 Grocery List

Ingredients in italics are Pantry Staples (page 11), so you may have them already.

Meat and Fish

- 500 g beef chuck, blade or rump steak
- 500 g chicken mince
- 4 large bone-in, skin-on chicken thigh cutlets (1 kg)
- 250 g chicken breast fillet
- 250 g chorizo

Fruit and Veg

- 1 bunch green onions
- 5 brown onions
- 3 bulbs garlic
- 20 g fresh ginger
- 2 birds-eye chillies
- 3 large carrots
- 2 lemons
- 400 g bag baby spinach
- 2 heads broccoli (roughly 900 g total)
- 1 large bunch basil
- 1 red capsicum
- 150 g green beans

Fridge and Freezer

- 300 ml thickened cream
- 50 g feta
- *plain Greek yoghurt*
- *parmesan*
- *unsalted butter*
- 4 eggs

Pantry

- 190 g jar basil pesto (gluten-free if required)
- 375 g pack red lentils
- 2 × 400 g tins butter beans
- 3 × 800 g tins diced or crushed tomatoes
- 1 × 400 g tin chickpeas
- 500 g penne
- loaf Turkish bread
- *olive oil*
- *vegetable oil*
- *salt*
- *pepper*
- *paprika*
- *dried oregano*
- *cayenne pepper*
- *ground cinnamon*
- *ground turmeric*
- *ground cumin*
- *ground coriander*
- *brown sugar*
- *jasmine rice*
- *basmati rice*
- *light soy sauce*
- *dark soy sauce*
- *rice wine vinegar*
- *oyster sauce*
- *fish sauce*
- *sriracha*
- *vegetable stock cubes/powder*
- *chicken stock cubes/powder*
- *cornflour*
- *bicarb soda*

Week 4 Swap 'n' Save

Some weeks the budget is tighter than others, or you're more busy, more tired, have unexpected guests, want to mix things up, or are catering for dietary preferences. Use the tips below to make adjustments to suit.

 Swap out

skin-on, bone-in chicken thigh cutlets ⟶ chicken drumsticks

chicken mince ⟶ pork mince

chicken breast fillet ⟶ chicken thigh fillet

beef chuck ⟶ beef stir-fry strips

chorizo ⟶ bacon

basil pesto ⟶ sun-dried tomato pesto

penne pasta ⟶ any pasta shape

Ⓢ Pocket some savings

Pesto: I've tested the pesto pasta recipe with home-brand pesto and it's delicious. You can't taste the difference, and it costs less than $2 – half the price of the branded products.

Chorizo: Often on special in the deli at the two major supermarkets – buy a few and freeze for up to 3 months.

Onions: If green onions are quite expensive or difficult to source, use 1 brown onion in each of the stir-fry recipes as a substitute.

Beef: I aim to spend around $15 per kg when purchasing beef for stir-fries. The cheapest cuts in the supermarkets are usually chuck or blade but, as 'braising' cuts, will need a little longer in the marinade to tenderise, if using for stir-fry. I will often portion up a beef blade or chuck roast when on special and freeze or slow cook the remainder for another meal. Stir-fry strips are generally over $20 per kg, but are a great convenience option.

Ⓛ Leftovers

You may have some leftover basil pesto and/or fresh basil this week. If so, here are some ideas to ensure they don't go to waste.

- Use as a spread or garnish, to add flavour to sandwiches and toasties.
- Stir through scrambled eggs to make 'green eggs' and/or add to omelettes.
- Portion into ice-cube trays and freeze (add olive oil to encase the diced fresh herbs), so you can add to pasta sauces and to flavour other dishes as needed.

Chicken Pesto Pasta

Comforting creamy carbs with plenty of greens

SERVES 6
PREP 15 minutes
COOK 15 minutes

1 brown onion, diced
4 cloves garlic, crushed
1 head broccoli (400–500 g),
    chopped into small florets
250 g chicken breast fillet,
    sliced into thin pieces
500 g penne
1 tablespoon unsalted butter
1 teaspoon olive oil
½ cup (130 g) basil pesto
300 ml thickened cream
½ cup (40 g) finely grated parmesan
¼ teaspoon ground black pepper
1 chicken stock cube
130 g baby spinach

To serve
2 tablespoons fresh basil leaves,
    thinly sliced
finely grated parmesan

PREP

✓ Put a large pot of salted water on to boil, ensuring that there is enough water to cover both the pasta and broccoli.

✓ Dice the onion, crush the garlic and chop the broccoli into small florets.

✓ Slice the chicken breast into thin pieces or small cubes.

COOK

1. Tip the pasta into the pot of boiling water. While the pasta is cooking, melt the butter with the oil in a large frying pan over medium heat. Add the onion and cook for a few minutes, until soft. Add the garlic and cook for another minute.

2. Add the chicken to the pan and cook for 4–5 minutes or until lightly browned and cooked through. Reduce the heat to low. Stir in the pesto, then add the cream and parmesan, stirring to combine. Add pepper, then crumble the stock cube into the sauce. Stir the spinach through until wilted and the sauce has heated through.

3. When the pasta is 2 minutes away from al dente, add the broccoli to the pot and cook for a minute or two. Scoop out ½ cup (125 ml) of pasta water and set it aside.

4. Drain the pasta and broccoli in a large colander. If your frying pan is large enough, add the pasta and broccoli to the sauce. If not, transfer the sauce, pasta and broccoli into the large pot. Gently stir to combine everything together. Add ¼ cup (60 ml) of the pasta water, stirring to loosen the mixture, adding more water if necessary.

5. To serve, divide among bowls and top with basil leaves, parmesan and pepper.

NOTES

Gluten-free: Choose a gluten-free pasta and ensure your basil pesto is gluten-free.

Leftovers: Store in the fridge for up to 3 days. Reheat in the microwave or on the stovetop. This meal isn't suitable for freezing.

Pasta: Any pasta can be used for this recipe, but I recommend penne, rigatoni, farfalle or fusilli.

Substitutions: Use sun-dried tomato pesto in place of the basil pesto for a different spin on this recipe.

Vegetables: Zucchini and cherry tomatoes work well in this recipe, either replacing or together with the broccoli and spinach.

Chorizo and Lentil Soup

Light on spice, heavy on comfort

250 g fresh chorizo, diced
2 brown onions, diced
3 large carrots, diced
4 cloves garlic, crushed
375 g pack red lentils,
    rinsed well in sieve or colander
2 tablespoons olive oil
1 teaspoon salt
2 teaspoons ground cumin
1 teaspoon dried oregano
1 teaspoon paprika
2 × 800 g tins diced or crushed
    tomatoes
8 cups (2 litres) chicken or vegetable
    stock, plus extra if needed

To serve

finely grated zest and juice of 1 lemon
50 g feta, crumbled
toasted or grilled Turkish bread

PREP

✓ Dice the chorizo, onions and carrots, crush the garlic.

✓ Rinse the lentils well in a large sieve under cold, running water. Remove any discoloured pieces.

COOK

1. Heat the oil in a large pot over medium-high heat. Add the chorizo and cook for about 5 minutes, until browned. Use a slotted spoon to transfer the chorizo to a plate, leaving the flavoured oil in the pot.

2. Turn the heat down to medium and cook the onion and carrot in the chorizo-flavoured oil for a few minutes, stirring occasionally, until soft. Add the garlic, salt, cumin, oregano and paprika and stir for 1 minute.

3. Pour in the tomatoes and stock, then add the lentils and bring just to the boil. Reduce the heat to low allowing the mixture to simmer, partially covered, for about 20 minutes or until the lentils are soft. Stir occasionally to ensure that the lentils don't stick to the bottom of the pot.

4. If you like, use a stick blender to partially blend the soup. This thickens it but still leaves tiny chunks of veggies and lentils. Add in extra stock at this point if you feel that it's too thick.

5. Add most of the chorizo to the soup, reserving some to serve. Taste soup and season with salt and pepper.

6. To serve, ladle soup into bowls, add a squeeze of lemon juice and top with remaining chorizo, lemon zest and crumbled feta. Serve with grilled Turkish bread.

WEEK 4

NOTES

Chorizo: 250 g is usually 2 chorizo sausages. Choose a fresh or semi-cured chorizo that requires cooking, rather than a cured chorizo that can be eaten raw (like salami).

Dietaries: For gluten-free, ensure that the chorizo does not contain gluten. Omit the Turkish bread or replace with gluten-free bread, to serve. For dairy-free, omit the feta.

Leftovers: Store in the fridge for up to 3 days or freeze for up to 3 months. Reheat on the stovetop or in the microwave.

Spices: This isn't a spicy soup, but if your family prefers mild flavours, halve the spice quantities the first time you make this.

Mongolian Beef

A saucy Chinese takeaway classic

Marinated meat
500 g beef chuck, blade or rump steak
½ teaspoon bicarb soda
1 tablespoon cornflour
1 tablespoon light soy sauce
1 teaspoon vegetable oil

Sauce
2 tablespoons cornflour
½ cup (125 ml) chicken stock
⅓ cup (80 ml) light soy sauce
2 tablespoons dark soy sauce
1 teaspoon rice wine vinegar
⅓ cup (75 g) brown sugar,
   plus more to taste
½ teaspoon sriracha

Stir-fry
4 cloves garlic, crushed
1 tablespoon finely grated fresh ginger
1 head broccoli, chopped into florets
3 green onions
¼ cup (60 ml) vegetable oil

To serve
steamed jasmine rice

PREP

✓ For the **marinated meat**, trim the fat from the beef and slice it against the grain into thin strips (3 mm wide). Add beef strips to a bowl with the rest of the marinade ingredients and 1 tablespoon water. Mix together well. Cover and refrigerate for at least 1 hour, up to 24 hours.

✓ To make the **sauce**, place the cornflour into a bowl and gradually add the chicken stock, stirring until smooth. Stir in the remaining ingredients. Taste and add a bit more sugar if you prefer a sweeter sauce, then set aside.

✓ Crush the garlic, grate the ginger and chop the broccoli into florets for the **stir-fry**. Thinly slice the light part of the green onions and cut the dark green part into 5 cm pieces.

✓ Just before you're ready to cook, take the beef out of the fridge to bring it closer to room temp. You might also want to put your rice on now, so it's ready in time.

COOK

1. Heat a large wok or frying pan over high heat then add 2 tablespoons oil. Add half the beef, spreading it out in the wok and sear for about 30 seconds each side. Transfer to a plate, heat a little more oil if needed and cook remaining beef.

2. Bring the heat back up to high and add the remaining oil. Add the garlic, ginger and the pale parts of the green onion and stir-fry for 30 seconds. Add the broccoli and stir-fry for another 30 seconds.

3. Give the sauce a quick stir to recombine the ingredients, then add to the wok. Cook, stirring, for 1–2 minutes or until the sauce has thickened. Return the beef to the wok. Toss to coat the beef and vegetables in the sauce – it should be thick and glossy. Add half of the dark green onion parts.

4. To serve, divide rice among bowls and top with stir-fry beef. Garnish with the remaining green onion.

NOTES

Beef: Budget cuts, like chuck and blade, will benefit from a longer marinating time to tenderise the beef. If you're using rump or stir-fry strips, 30 minutes will suffice.

Gluten-free: Use tamari or gluten-free soy sauce in marinade. Use ½ cup (125 ml) tamari or gluten-free soy sauce in place of the light and dark soy sauces in the sauce mixture.

Leftovers: Store in the fridge for up to 2 days, then reheat in the microwave to serve. This recipe is not suitable for freezing.

Meat: You can make this dish with lamb, pork or chicken. Leave the bicarb soda out of the marinade if using chicken.

Spice: Taste the sauce prior to serving and add sriracha according

to your preference. If your family doesn't like spicy heat, start with ½ teaspoon sriracha or leave it out altogether – people can add their own upon serving.

Vegetables: Add extra vegetables to stretch this meal further. I recommend carrots, capsicum, snow peas and/or green beans – either fresh or frozen.

Middle Eastern Chicken and Rice

Fragrant one-pan wonder

Chicken marinade

2 cloves garlic, crushed
½ lemon, juiced
¼ cup (60 ml) olive oil
1 teaspoon salt
2 teaspoons ground cumin
2 teaspoons ground coriander
1 teaspoon paprika
1 teaspoon ground turmeric
½ teaspoon cayenne pepper
¼ teaspoon ground cinnamon
¼ teaspoon ground black pepper
4 large skin-on, bone-in chicken thigh
   cutlets

Spiced rice and chickpeas

½ large brown onion, finely diced
2 large cloves garlic, crushed
400 g tin chickpeas, rinsed and drained
1 tablespoon olive oil
40 g unsalted butter
¼ teaspoon ground cinnamon
¼ teaspoon ground cumin
¼ teaspoon ground turmeric
130 g baby spinach
1½ cups (300 g) basmati rice,
   rinsed well
3 cups (750 ml) gluten-free
   chicken stock
½ lemon, thinly sliced

To serve

plain Greek yoghurt

PREP

✓ Between 1 to 24 hours ahead of cooking, marinate the chicken. To prepare the chicken marinade, crush the garlic, juice the lemon and mix together with the remaining marinade ingredients in a large bowl or shallow dish. Add chicken and stir well to coat. Cover and refrigerate for a minimum of 1 hour (up to 24).

✓ For the spiced rice and chickpeas, finely dice onion, cover and set aside until ready to use in main dish. Crush another 2 cloves of garlic, cover and set aside until ready to use in main dish.

✓ When ready to cook, preheat the oven to 180°C, then remove the marinated chicken from the fridge. Drain the chickpeas in a sieve and rinse until water runs clear.

COOK

1. Heat the oil in a large flameproof and ovenproof pan over medium-high heat. Add the chicken to the pan (reserving the marinade) and cook for 5–7 minutes each side, until browned.

2. Set chicken aside on a plate. Reduce the heat to medium-low, removing any large, blackened residue from the flavoured oil.

3. Add butter (substitute oil for dairy-free) to the pan. Once melted, add the onion and cook for a few minutes, stirring until soft. Add the garlic, spices and spinach and stir until wilted. Pour in the reserved chicken marinade and add the rice. Stir well so that the rice is coated with the onion, spices and marinade.

4. Stir in the stock and turn the heat up to medium. Once it starts simmering, turn the heat off. Stir in the chickpeas then arrange the chicken pieces on top of the rice. Cover with a lid or a double layer of foil and pop it in the oven to cook for 30 minutes.

5. Remove the lid or foil, arrange the thinly sliced lemon on top, turn up the heat to 200°C and cook for another 5–10 minutes, until chicken is cooked. (The chicken is ready when you prick it with a skewer and its juices run clear, or when its internal temperature reaches 75°C when tested with a meat thermometer. If in doubt, cut a piece to check it's completely cooked through and not still pink in the middle.) If you want to brown the chicken further, pop it under the grill for a few minutes.

6. Serve as is, or with a dollop of plain Greek yoghurt. This is also delicious with a fresh side salad like tabbouli.

NOTES

Chicken: If you want to increase the amount of chicken, you can generally fit 6–8 pieces of chicken in the pan. Since it's the rice that absorbs the water, there's no need to make any further adjustments. Drumsticks can be used instead of thighs.

Dairy-free: Replace the butter with 1 tablespoon olive oil, and leave off the yoghurt to serve.

Leftovers: Store in the fridge for up to 2 days or freeze for up to 1 month. Reheat in the microwave.

Pan: I usually cook this in a lidded, ceramic-lined French pan. If you don't have an ovenproof pan that you can also use on the stove, transfer the rice to a baking dish once it's started simmering. Place the chicken on top, cover and bake.

Thai Basil Chicken Stir-Fry

Better than takeaway (and faster too!)

Sauce

1 tablespoon cornflour
¼ cup (60 ml) chicken stock
1 tablespoon light soy sauce
1 tablespoon oyster sauce
1 teaspoon fish sauce
2 teaspoons brown sugar

Stir-fry

1 red capsicum, diced
150 g green beans, trimmed and
   sliced into 3 cm pieces
3 green onions, thinly sliced
   (pale part only)
5 cloves garlic, crushed
1 birds-eye chilli, finely chopped
2 tablespoons vegetable oil
500 g chicken mince
1 cup basil leaves, loosely packed

To serve

steamed jasmine rice
4 fried eggs
basil leaves
sliced fresh chilli

PREP

✓ To make the **sauce**, place the cornflour into a bowl or jug and gradually add the chicken stock, stirring until smooth. Stir in the remaining ingredients and set aside.

✓ For the **stir-fry**, dice the capsicum, slice the green beans and the green onions. Crush the garlic and finely chop the chilli.

✓ Put the rice on about 20 minutes before cooking the stir-fry.

COOK

1. Heat a wok or large frying pan over high heat then add 1 tablespoon oil. When the oil is hot, stir-fry the garlic, chilli and green onion for 30 seconds. Add the capsicum and green beans, stir-fry for 1 minute, then transfer to a plate.

2. Bring the wok back up to high heat then add the remaining oil. Add the chicken mince, spread it out into a thin layer and let it sear for a couple of minutes. Break it up into small pieces and stir-fry for a few minutes, until browned through.

3. While this is cooking, fry the eggs in another pan. Once cooked, set aside.

4. Return the vegetables to the wok. Give the sauce a quick stir to combine and pour over the vegetables. Stir-fry for another couple of minutes to combine everything and thicken the sauce. Toss the basil through. Taste and adjust spice and sugar levels, then turn off the heat.

5. To serve, divide rice among bowls and top with stir-fry and a fried egg. Sprinkle with the extra basil and chilli.

NOTES

Basil: Thai basil would usually be the preferred and authentic choice for this dish. Because we're using sweet basil in two other recipes this week, we're using it for this dish also.

Chilli: Always be careful when handling chilli – use gloves or wash your hands very well after slicing or touching. Do not touch or rub your eyes! If you want a milder dish, start with one de-seeded chilli, or substitute by adding sriracha, ½ teaspoon at a time.

Gluten-free: Substitute tamari or gluten-free soy sauce for the light soy sauce, and make sure the oyster sauce is gluten-free.

Leftovers: Store in the fridge for up to 2 days (without the egg) and reheat in the microwave. I don't recommend freezing this dish.

Butter Bean Stew

A hearty and decadent stew of golden beans

1 brown onion, diced
3 large cloves garlic, crushed
2 × 400 g tins butter beans,
    rinsed and drained
2 tablespoons olive oil
2 teaspoons dried oregano
2 teaspoons paprika
800 g tin diced or crushed tomatoes
½ cup (125 ml) vegetable stock
140 g baby spinach
handful fresh basil leaves, sliced

To serve
½ lemon
grated or shaved parmesan
fresh basil leaves
garlic bread or crusty bread

PREP

✓ Dice the onion and crush the garlic, keeping them separate.

✓ Drain the butter beans in a sieve or colander and rinse until the water runs clear.

COOK

1. Heat the oil in a large frying pan or saucepan over medium-low heat. Add the onion and cook, stirring, for a few minutes until soft. Add the garlic and cook for another minute. Add the oregano and paprika and cook, stirring, for 30 seconds.

2. Pour in the tomatoes and stock. Bring to a simmer and cook uncovered for 5–10 minutes, to develop the flavour. Season with salt and pepper to taste.

3. Add the butter beans and spinach. Gently fold into the tomato sauce, being careful not to crush the butter beans. Simmer for another 5 minutes or until heated through. Stir the sliced basil leaves through, then taste and season again if necessary.

4. To serve, spoon into bowls and give each a squeeze of lemon juice. Top with parmesan and extra basil. Serve with crusty bread or garlic bread.

NOTES

Dietaries: For dairy-free, omit the parmesan. While butter beans are velvety and decadent, they don't contain any butter (dairy) so you're safe there. For gluten-free, replace the bread with gluten-free bread.

Leftovers: Store in the fridge for up to 3 days or in the freezer for up to 3 months. Reheat in the microwave or on the stovetop.

Meat: You can add a bit of extra flavour and satisfy the meat lovers in your family by frying bacon or chorizo first. Once cooked, remove and set aside. Cook the onion in the leftover oil (for added flavour). Add the bacon or chorizo back in with the butter beans.

Seasoning: Italian seasoning can be used in place of the paprika and oregano. You could also add some dried chilli flakes for an extra kick.

Vegetarian: To keep this vegetarian, stick with using vegetable stock. However, if this is not a concern, chicken stock works fine too.

Beef It Up

Week 5

Sunday

Beef Burrito Bowls

Monday

Chicken Paprikash

Tuesday

Black Pepper Beef

Wednesday

Beef 'n' Bean Nachos

Thursday

Veggie Tagine

Friday

Chicken Pad See Ew

Saturday

Veggie Tagine

Week 5 at a Glance

 **28 meals**
plus 5 leftovers

 **$2.50**
per serving

The showstopper base recipe this week is the slow cooked Mexican Beef which delivers on flavour for Sunday's Beef Burrito Bowls and Wednesday's Beef 'n' Bean Nachos. To supplement the cost of the beef, we have 5 nights of low-cost meals that are no less impressive or appetising!

Sunday

It's worth dragging your slow cooker out of storage for the slow cooked Beef Burrito Bowls, but you can also cook it in your oven. You'll need to cut off a third (500 g) of the beef roast for Tuesday's stir-fry. If you have time, thinly slice that portion now (against the grain) and pop it in the fridge. For deliciously tender beef, slow cook it on low for 9 hours then serve with your choice of rice, salad and garnishes. You'll need to refrigerate about 1½ cups of the beef in a container for the Beef 'n' Bean Nachos on Wednesday. Keep any excess slow cooker juices in a separate container – they're packed with flavour and you may want to add a little more liquid to the beef when you reheat it.

Monday

Chicken Paprikash is a traditional Hungarian recipe that may not have come across your radar until now. The combination of paprika, tomato and sour cream results in a flavoursome sauce that coats the chicken, with plenty left to drizzle over your carby side of choice. 500 g rigatoni is included in the grocery list, but any pasta can be used. Alternatively, mashed or cubed boiled potatoes are an excellent gluten-free accompaniment.

Tuesday

This Black Pepper Beef is my favourite beef stir-fry, hands down. Marinate the beef at least 1 hour ahead of cooking to guarantee beautifully soft, silky meat. It's a very quick meal to make so remember to put the rice on prior to cooking the stir-fry to ensure that they're ready at the same time. Keep any leftovers to reheat for lunch but you may be tempted to go back for seconds.

Wednesday

Tonight's Beef 'n' Bean Nachos will be ready in under 30 minutes. If you have room in the budget, buy a cheap salsa so you have something else to dip your corn chips into. You can put as little or as much effort as you want into the toppings. Use the recipe as a guide – it's nachos – unless you burn it, you can't really stuff it up!

Thursday

You'll cook a double batch of this vegan Veggie Tagine tonight and it's up to you whether you freeze the remaining portions or keep them for Saturday night's dinner. You have the option of serving it with basmati rice or couscous. The vegetables listed in the recipe and grocery list are suggestions. If you have remnants in your fridge or pantry that you want to use up, use them first then choose from seasonal, cheap options when you shop. You're aiming for a minimum of 8 cups of vegetables for this recipe.

Friday

Once you make this Chicken Pad See Ew for yourself, you'll have a really hard time paying $20+ for it at your local Thai takeaway! It is so quick to make and most of the ingredients are pantry staples. It's also one of the milder stir-fry sauces in this book, making it very child-friendly. Replace the chicken with your protein of choice for something different, and use any Asian green veg.

Saturday

You might already have plans for tonight to eat out but if not, you can heat up the Veggie Tagine and make a fresh batch of rice or couscous.

Week 5 Grocery List

Ingredients in italics are Pantry Staples (page 11), so you may have them already.

Meat and Fish

- 1.5k g beef chuck or blade roast
- 6–8 skin-on, bone-in chicken pieces (thighs or drumsticks, about 1.5 kg)
- 250 g chicken breast

Fruit and Veg

- 1 bunch green onions
- 6 brown onions
- 1 small red onion
- 3 bulbs garlic
- 25 g fresh ginger
- 2 large carrots
- 4 limes
- 1 lemon
- 2 large avocados
- 200 g bag coleslaw mix
- 4 red capsicums
- 1 green capsicum
- 200 g green beans
- 1 bunch gai lan (Chinese broccoli)
- ½ cauliflower
- 1 large zucchini
- 1 medium or 2 small sweet potatoes
- 1 large bunch coriander
- 4 large tomatoes

Fridge and Freezer

- 125 g grated Mexican cheese
- 300 g sour cream
- *plain Greek yoghurt*
- *unsalted butter*
- *4 eggs*

Pantry

- 2 × 200 g packs dried pad thai noodles
- 2 × 400 g tins chickpeas
- 200 g pack corn or tortilla chips
- 3 × 400 g tins diced or crushed tomatoes
- 2 × 400 g tins black beans
- 1 × 400 g tin corn kernels
- 500 g couscous (optional)
- 500 g rigatoni
- *basmati rice*
- *bicarb soda*
- *pepper*
- *brown sugar*
- *caster sugar*
- *cayenne pepper*
- *cornflour*
- *dark soy sauce*
- *dried oregano*
- *fish sauce*
- *garlic powder*
- *ground cinnamon*
- *ground coriander*
- *ground cumin*
- *ground turmeric*
- *honey*
- *jasmine rice*
- *light soy sauce*
- *mayonnaise*
- *olive oil*
- *oyster sauce*
- *paprika*
- *rice wine vinegar*
- *salt*
- *sesame oil*
- *sriracha*
- *tomato paste*
- *veg, beef and chicken stock cubes/powder*
- *vegetable oil*
- *white vinegar*

Week 5 Swap 'n' Save

Some weeks the budget is tighter than others, or you're more busy, more tired, have unexpected guests, want to mix things up, or are catering for dietary preferences. Use the tips below to make adjustments to suit.

 Swap out

chicken breast ⟶ boneless chicken thigh

gai lan ⟶ any Asian veg, broccoli or broccolini

grated Mexican cheese ⟶ any melting cheese

rigatoni ⟶ any pasta shape or 800 g potatoes

coleslaw ⟶ iceberg lettuce

2 × 200 g dried pad thai noodles ⟶ 750–800 g fresh wide rice noodles

400 g tin black beans ⟶ 400 g tin kidney beans

Pocket some savings

Capsicum: The only capsicum that is essential is the 1 red capsicum used for the Chicken Paprikash. If they're expensive, swap the others out for any affordable stir-fry vegetables.

Chicken: If you're comfortable portioning up a whole chicken (into 8 pieces) it's usually cheaper than buying the pieces separately for the Paprikash. Drumsticks will always be the best value cut of chicken at $5 or less per kg.

Veggies: Audit your crisper and pantry and see what you have leftover prior to finalising your grocery list. The Veggie Tagine is so versatile. Any veggie that works well in a soup or curry can be used for this recipe. You'll need around 8 cups of chopped veggies to yield 8 servings.

Choices, choices

Pad thai rice noodles: Try to find the widest dried rice noodles available to you. The major supermarkets and Amazon stock the Erawan brand noodles. Other brands can be purchased at Asian grocers. If you would prefer to use fresh rice noodles, they can also be found at Asian grocers. Some supermarkets also stock them in the fridges, usually alongside fresh egg noodles and dumpling wrappers.

Corn chips: I buy the triangular, lightly salted home brand corn chips for my nachos. I find that they're thick enough that they hold their shape and don't go soggy … and they're really cheap!

 Leftovers

If you cook the meal plan as written, there shouldn't be any leftover ingredients aside from the pantry staples.

Slow Cooker Mexican Beef

Tender meat, loaded with flavour

400 g tin diced or crushed tomatoes
1 beef stock cube, crumbled
juice of 1 lime
2 tablespoons brown sugar
2 brown onions, sliced
2 cloves garlic, smashed
1 kg beef chuck or blade roast

Dry rub

2 teaspoons paprika
2 teaspoons dried oregano
2 teaspoons ground cumin
2 teaspoons garlic powder
2 teaspoons salt
½ teaspoon ground black pepper
¼–½ teaspoon cayenne pepper

PREP

✓ To make the dry rub, mix the ingredients together in a small bowl.

✓ Combine the tomatoes, stock cube, lime juice and brown sugar in a medium bowl or jug.

COOK

1. Turn on the slow cooker and set to low or high.

2. Spread the onion and garlic over the base of the slow cooker. Rub the dry rub all over the meat and place on top of the onion.

3. Gently pour the tomato mixture over the meat and add any remaining dry rub. Cover and cook on low for 9 hours or high for 5 hours. The meat should be fall-apart tender.

4. Transfer meat to a large bowl and shred with 2 forks. Remove 1 cup of the slow cooker liquid and put it into a container in the fridge. Return the shredded beef to the slow cooker and mix through the remaining cooking liquid. Taste and add a little more salt or brown sugar if necessary.

5. Serve as filling for any Mexican dish such as the Beef Burrito Bowls or Beef 'n' Bean Nachos in this meal plan, or use in tacos or on baked potatoes.

NOTES

Consistency: Depending on what you're using the beef for, you may want a drier or wetter consistency. Add some of the reserved liquid (or additional beef stock) as needed, particularly when reheating.

Leftovers: Store in the fridge for up to 3 days. Reheat in the microwave or on the stovetop in a frying pan. Freeze for up to 1 month.

Meal plan: If cooking as part of the meal plan, reserve about 1½ cups of the shredded beef for the Beef 'n' Bean Nachos and use the rest for the Beef Burrito Bowls.

Spice: This can be made without the cayenne pepper but I suggest starting with ¼ teaspoon.

Stove top: To make this without a slow cooker, prep as instructed, slice the beef into 3–4 pieces and brown in batches in a large pan over medium-high heat. Set aside. Cook onions and garlic in 1 tablespoon olive oil in the pan for a few minutes. Turn heat down to low, add the dry rub spices, tomatoes, stock cube, lime juice, sugar and 1 cup (250 ml) water. Return beef to pan and simmer, covered, for 2 hours. Check after 1 hour and add additional water or stock if needed.

Beef Burrito Bowls

Vibrant and well-balanced

Steamed rice
3 cups Slow Cooker Mexican Beef
  (page 106), heated
400 g tin black beans, rinsed and
  drained (optional)
400 g tin corn kernels, drained

Mexican coleslaw

200 g coleslaw mix
1 tablespoon finely chopped coriander
2 tablespoons mayonnaise
1 teaspoon white vinegar
squeeze lime juice, to taste
½ teaspoon caster sugar
¼ teaspoon salt

Pico de gallo

2 tomatoes, diced
2 tablespoons finely chopped
  coriander leaves
2 tablespoons finely diced red onion
1 tablespoon lime juice
¼ teaspoon salt

Guacamole

1 large avocado, gently mashed
1 tablespoon finely chopped coriander
  leaves
1 tablespoon finely diced red onion
2 teaspoons lime juice
¼ teaspoon salt

To serve

sour cream
coriander leaves

STEPS

1. To make the Mexican coleslaw, tip the coleslaw mix into a bowl and add the coriander. Combine the remaining ingredients and toss through the slaw. Pop it into the fridge until you're ready to assemble the bowls.

2. For the pico de gallo and guacamole, combine the ingredients in separate bowls. Taste and adjust flavour by adding salt or lime juice if needed.

3. Divide the coleslaw, rice, beef, beans (if using), corn and pico de gallo between bowls.

4. Dollop with sour cream and guacamole, and top with coriander leaves.

NOTES

Dairy-free: Leave off the sour cream.

Flavour boost: Mix a pinch of salt, a squeeze of lime and some finely chopped coriander into the sour cream for an easy lime crema. Mix finely chopped coriander and a good squeeze of lime juice through the rice.

Leftovers: Store in the fridge for up to 2 days. Reheat the beef and rice in the microwave or on the stovetop.

Substitutions: To change up the Burrito Bowls, swap out the beef for 600–800 g diced chicken seasoned with a Mexican spice mix and cooked in a frying pan.

Timing: I recommend starting on the rice when the beef is just about ready and shred the beef just before serving. While the rice is cooking you can prepare the pico di gallo, guacamole and coleslaw.

Chicken Paprikash

Hungarian comfort food at its best

1 large brown onion, thinly sliced
1 red capsicum, thinly sliced
4 cloves garlic, crushed
6–8 large skin-on, bone-in chicken pieces (thighs or drumsticks)
15 g butter
1 tablespoon olive oil
3 tablespoons paprika
1 tablespoon tomato paste
400 g tin diced or crushed tomatoes
2 cups (500 ml) chicken stock
2 teaspoons cornflour
½ cup (120 g) sour cream

To serve
500 g rigatoni

PREP

✓ Slice the onion and capsicum, crush the garlic.

✓ Season chicken well with salt and pepper.

COOK

1. Heat the butter and oil in a large frying pan (you'll need a lid for it later) over medium-high heat. Cook the chicken skin-side down for a few minutes or until browned, then turn and cook on the other side for a few minutes. Remove from the pan and set aside on a plate.

2. Add the onion to the pan and cook, stirring, for a few minutes until soft. Add the capsicum and garlic and cook, stirring, for another couple of minutes. Remove from the heat and stir in the paprika. Add the tomato paste to the pan, stir through then place back on the heat, cooking for a couple of minutes.

3. Add the tomatoes and chicken stock and bring to a simmer. Reduce heat to low and add the chicken pieces back to the pan.

4. Cook, partially covered, for at least 30 minutes or until the chicken is well cooked through. While the chicken is cooking, bring a large pot of water to the boil. 10 minutes before the chicken is ready, cook the pasta.

5. Stir the cornflour and sour cream together in a small bowl. Remove the chicken from the sauce and set aside on a plate. Take the pan off the heat and stir the sour cream mixture through the sauce. Add the chicken back in and coat well in the sauce. Put the pan back on low heat and simmer for a couple of minutes to thicken the sauce. Serve with the pasta.

NOTES

Chicken: I cook 1 chicken thigh cutlet per person or 1–2 chicken drumsticks per person. When the chicken is removed from the pan you can shred it for those who prefer boneless chicken.

Flavour boost: Add a pinch of cayenne pepper with the paprika for a hint of spice.

Gluten-free: Serve with gluten-free pasta.

Leftovers: Store in the fridge for up to 2 days. Freeze for up to 2 months. Reheat in the microwave or on the stovetop.

Sauce: If your family doesn't like large pieces of capsicum or onion, dice them up finely instead of slicing them or leave out the capsicum altogether. You could also blend the sauce, before you add the sour cream.

Black Pepper Beef

My favourite stir-fry, hands down!

3 tablespoons vegetable oil
1 brown onion, thinly sliced
3 cloves garlic, crushed
2 teaspoons finely grated fresh ginger
2 red capsicums, thinly sliced
1 green capsicum, thinly sliced
200 g green beans, trimmed and
 halved

Marinated meat

500 g beef chuck or blade roast
½ teaspoon bicarb soda
1 tablespoon cornflour
1 tablespoon light soy sauce
1 teaspoon sesame oil
¼ teaspoon coarsely ground
 black pepper

Sauce

1 tablespoon cornflour
3 tablespoons oyster sauce
2 teaspoons light soy sauce
1 teaspoon dark soy sauce
2 teaspoons rice wine vinegar
1 teaspoon brown sugar
½ teaspoon coarsely ground black
 pepper

To serve

steamed jasmine rice

PREP

✓ For the marinated meat, trim any fat and slice it against the grain into thin strips (3–4 mm). Place into a large bowl with the rest of the marinade ingredients and 2 tablespoons water. Mix together well. Cover and refrigerate for 1 hour or up to 24 hours.

✓ Just before you're ready to cook, take the beef out of the fridge to bring it closer to room temperature. (This is a good time to cook the rice.)

✓ For the sauce, place the cornflour into a bowl and gradually add ¼ cup (60 ml) water, stirring until smooth. Stir in the remaining ingredients.

COOK

1. Heat a large wok or frying pan over high heat then add 1 ½ tablespoons oil. Add half the beef, spreading it out in the wok, and sear for about 30 seconds each side, until browned. Transfer to a plate, heat a little extra oil if needed and cook the remaining beef in the same way.

2. Bring the heat back up to high and add the remaining oil if there's not much left. Add the onion, garlic and ginger and stir-fry for 30 seconds. Add the capsicum and beans and stir-fry for 2 minutes.

3. Give the sauce a quick stir to combine the ingredients again then add to the wok. Cook, stirring, for 1–2 minutes, or until the sauce has thickened. Return the beef to the wok. Toss to coat the meat and vegetables in the sauce – it should be thick and glossy. Add 1–2 tablespoons water if it becomes too thick. Serve in bowls over rice.

WEEK 5

NOTES

Beef: Budget cuts like chuck and blade will benefit from a longer marinating time to tenderise the beef. If you're using rump or pre-cut stir-fry strips, 30 minutes will suffice.

Gluten-free: Use tamari or gluten-free soy sauce in marinade. Use 3 teaspoons tamari or gluten-free soy sauce in place of the light and dark soy sauces in the sauce mixture. Make sure the oyster sauce is gluten-free.

Leftovers: Store in the fridge for up to 2 days, reheat in the microwave. This recipe is not suitable for freezing.

Meat: You can make this dish with lamb, pork or chicken. Leave out the bicarb soda if using chicken.

Pepper: If you can't get enough of the pepper flavour, taste and add more in just before serving. You can also reduce the pepper in the sauce to ¼ teaspoon

or omit it altogether if you're concerned about the level of heat.

Vegetables: Add extra vegetables to stretch this meal further. I recommend carrots, snow peas or broccoli – either fresh or frozen.

Beef 'n' Bean Nachos

The freshest tasting nachos I've eaten

PREP 15 minutes
COOK 15 minutes

200 g pack corn or tortilla chips
1¼ cups (125 g) Mexican shredded
cheese
1½ cups Slow Cooker Mexican Beef
(page 106)
400 g tin black beans, rinsed and
drained

Pico de gallo

2 tomatoes, diced
2 tablespoons finely chopped
coriander leaves
2 tablespoons finely diced red onion
1 tablespoon lime juice
¼ teaspoon salt

Guacamole

1 large avocado, gently mashed
1 tablespoon finely chopped coriander
leaves
1 tablespoon finely diced red onion
2 teaspoons lime juice
¼ teaspoon salt

To serve

sour cream
coriander leaves
sliced green onion
lime wedges

PREP

✓ Preheat the oven to 190°C. Line a large baking tray with baking paper.

✓ For the pico de gallo and guacamole, combine the ingredients in separate bowls. Taste and adjust flavour by adding salt or lime juice if needed.

COOK

1. Arrange the corn chips in an even layer on the baking tray and sprinkle with ⅓ of the grated cheese. Bake for a few minutes, until the cheese has fully melted.

2. Meanwhile, heat the beef in the microwave or on the stovetop then stir through the black beans. If it is too thick and stodgy, add some of the reserved beef cooking liquid, 1 tablespoon at a time.

3. Remove the tray from the oven and spread the beef and bean mixture evenly over the corn chips. Sprinkle with the remaining cheese and put it back in the oven for about 8 minutes, until cheese has melted.

4. Remove the nachos from the oven. Top with pico de gallo. Dollop with guacamole and sour cream. Sprinkle with coriander leaves and green onion, and serve with lime wedges on the side.

NOTES

Cheese: Mexican shredded cheese is a pre-grated blend of cheeses. Just use tasty cheese if you like. I prefer fresh tasting nachos that aren't too weighed down by melted cheese or cheese sauce. However, if you love seriously cheesy nachos, feel free to add more.

Corn chips: Choose thick corn chips or tortilla chips. They won't get soggy and will hold their shape. You'll want the 'lightly salted' or 'plain' varieties for this recipe.

Leftovers: There won't be any . . . seriously!!

Veggie Tagine

A light Moroccan vegetable and chickpea stew

PREP **15 minutes**
COOK **1 hour**

2 brown onions, diced
4 large cloves garlic, crushed
1 teaspoon finely grated fresh ginger
2 large carrots, peeled and cut into
　1 cm slices
1 sweet potato, peeled and cut into
　2–3 cm cubes
1 large zucchini, cut into 2 cm slices
1 red capsicum, sliced
½ cauliflower, broken into small florets
1 teaspoon ground cumin
1 teaspoon ground cinnamon
1 teaspoon ground turmeric
1 teaspoon ground coriander
2 tablespoons olive oil
　(and more if needed)
1 teaspoon sriracha (or harissa paste)
400 g tin diced or crushed tomatoes
4 cups (1 litre) vegetable stock
1 tablespoon honey
2 × 400 g tins chickpeas,
　rinsed and drained
2 tablespoons chopped coriander
　leaves
juice of 1 lemon

To serve

steamed basmati rice or prepared
　couscous, to serve
plain Greek yoghurt

PREP

✓ Dice the onion, crush the garlic and grate the ginger.

✓ Peel and cut the carrots into 1 cm slices, peel the sweet potato and chop into 2–3 cm cubes.

✓ Cut the zucchini into 2 cm slices, slice the capsicum and break the cauliflower into florets.

✓ Combine the cumin, cinnamon, turmeric and coriander in a small bowl and set aside.

COOK

1. Heat the oil in a large heavy-based pan (that has a lid) over medium heat. Add the onion and cook, stirring, for a few minutes until soft. Add the garlic, ginger, combined spices and sriracha or harissa paste. Cook for 1–2 minutes, stirring constantly, until fragrant.

2. Add the carrot and sweet potato and stir until well covered in the onion mixture. You may need to add another tablespoon of oil at this point to prevent the ingredients from sticking to the pan.

3. Add the zucchini, capsicum and cauliflower. Cook, stirring gently, for a few minutes until starting to soften.

4. Add the tomatoes, stock and honey and mix through. Bring just to the boil then turn down to low so it's simmering gently. Cover and cook for 30–40 minutes or until all the vegetables are tender. (If serving with rice, start cooking it now.)

5. Remove lid, add chickpeas and simmer, uncovered, for 10 minutes. (If serving with couscous, prepare it now.) Taste and season well with salt and pepper.

6. Stir through the coriander and lemon juice. Serve over rice or couscous, with a dollop of yoghurt.

NOTES

Dietaries: For dairy-free, leave off the yoghurt. For gluten-free, serve with rice rather than couscous.

Flavour boost: A handful of diced dried apricots can be added in at step 5 for some extra flavour.

Leftovers: Store in the fridge for up to 3 days or the freezer for up to 3 months. Reheat on the stovetop or in the microwave.

Meat: You could sear 400 g of diced chicken thigh first, transfer to a bowl, then add back in at step 4 for some added protein.

Spice: This is quite a mild dish, but if you're wanting more spice and flavour you can double the amount of sriracha or harissa paste, or add ¼–½ teaspoon cayenne pepper. For a more punchy flavour, increase the spices to 1½ teaspoons each.

Vegetables: Use any vegetables that are in season or on special at the time. Pumpkin, potato, eggplant or green beans would all be great. Parsley can be used instead of coriander.

WEEK 5

WEEK 5 • BEEF IT UP　117

Chicken Pad See Ew

Pad thai's salty soy cousin

SERVES 5

PREP 15 minutes

COOK 15 minutes

400 g dried pad thai noodles
1 large bunch of gai lan
(Chinese broccoli)
3 tablespoons vegetable oil
4 cloves garlic, crushed
4 eggs, beaten

Marinated chicken

250 g chicken breast, thinly sliced
2 teaspoons light soy sauce
1 teaspoon vegetable oil
¼ teaspoon black pepper

Sauce

3 tablespoons oyster sauce
3 tablespoons dark soy sauce
1 tablespoon light soy sauce
1 tablespoon fish sauce
1½ tablespoons brown sugar

To serve

sliced green onion
lime wedges (optional)

PREP

✓ For the marinated chicken, place all the ingredients into a bowl and mix together well. Set aside.

✓ For the sauce, mix ingredients together in a bowl or jug.

✓ Place dried noodles in a large bowl and cover with boiling water. Let them soften for about 10 minutes. Check regularly and once they are softened but al dente, drain in a colander. Meanwhile, chop the gai lan stalks into 5 cm pieces and slice the leaves (keep separate).

COOK

1. Heat a wok or large frying pan over high heat then add 1 tablespoon oil. When oil is hot, add chicken and spread out over the bottom of the pan. Allow it to sear for a minute, then stir-fry for another minute or until cooked through. Transfer to a large plate.

2. Add 2 teaspoons oil to the wok, bring the heat back up to high and add garlic and gai lan stems. Stir-fry for 1–2 minutes then add the gai lan leaves and stir-fry for another minute or until wilted.

3. Push the gai lan to the side and tip in the beaten eggs. Let them cook for a few seconds then stir to scramble and mix through the vegetables. Transfer the gai lan and eggs to the plate with the chicken.

4. Bring the wok back up to very high heat then add remaining oil. Give the sauce a quick stir then add the noodles to the wok followed by the sauce. Toss gently for 1–2 minutes, to heat through and caramelise the noodles, coating them with the sauce.

5. Add the chicken, egg and gai lan back into the pan. Stir gently to coat all of the ingredients with the sauce. Stir-fry for another couple of minutes to heat through. Serve immediately, garnished with green onions and a squeeze of fresh lime if using.

NOTES

Gai lan: If you can't get your hands on gai lan (Chinese broccoli) you can substitute with choy sum, bok choy, broccolini or a small head of broccoli.

Gluten-free: Use tamari or gluten-free soy sauce in the marinade. Use 4 tablespoons tamari or gluten-free soy sauce in place of the light and dark soy sauces in the sauce mixture. Make sure the oyster sauce is gluten-free.

Leftovers: Store in the fridge for up to 2 days and reheat in the microwave or in the wok. I don't recommend freezing this dish.

Noodles: You can use fresh rice noodles instead of the dried variety. These can be found at Asian grocers and some major supermarkets. You will need about 750–800 g fresh noodles for this recipe.

Protein: Substitute the chicken with tofu, beef or pork.

Sauce: If you like very saucy noodles, you can increase the oyster and dark soy sauces to ¼ cup, light soy and fish sauce to 1½ tablespoons and sugar to 2 tablespoons.

Spice: Add sriracha, sambal oelek, chilli oil or fresh chilli for some heat, either just before serving or at the table.

Cosy Cooking

Week 6

Sunday

Slow Cooked Greek Lamb

Monday

Spiced Lamb and
Eggplant Farfalle

Tuesday

Thai Red Chicken Curry

Wednesday

Lamb Harira

Thursday

Roasted Pumpkin Soup

Friday

Chicken Lo Mein

Saturday

Roasted Pumpkin Soup

Week 6 at a Glance

 **Servings: 28**
plus 8 leftovers

 $2.48
per serve

This is a full week of winter warmers that I serve up all year round in my home. It might surprise you that my favourite meal on this plan is not the hearty, succulent Slow Cooked Greek Lamb, but a dish made from its leftovers – the Lamb Harira, which is a thick Moroccan-style stew. It's a fragrant, comforting dish that I crave regularly and am never disappointed by! You'll also use leftover roast meat for the Spiced Lamb and Eggplant Farfalle, a fusion dish that is oddly delicious. Sunday is leftovers night and you can choose between the Pumpkin Soup, Lamb Harira and Thai Red Chicken Curry because you've got lots of leftovers this week!

Sunday

For the Slow Cooked Greek Lamb, you'll roast a 2.5 kg lamb leg which should yield around 1.5 kg of melt-in-your-mouth meat. You'll need to allow at least 6 ½ hours from starting your prep to serving this up, so plan ahead. The grocery list also includes ingredients for the Greek Lemon Potatoes and Green Beans and a batch of Tzatziki. You'll also have enough yoghurt to make flatbreads if you wish. Once the lamb is cooked, set aside at least 200 g of lamb and the bone for the Lamb Harira and 200 g for the Spiced Lamb and Eggplant Farfalle. If you have any additional leftover meat, save it for the Lamb Harira – the more the better.

Monday

Tonight's Spiced Lamb and Eggplant Farfalle is served with a yoghurt sauce and topped with fresh mint and crumbled feta. Do not leave any of these out, they take the dish from 'nice' to 'ohhhh yesss'! If you can't find or don't like eggplant, you can substitute it with zucchini and skip the roasting step.

Tuesday

You'll make 8 servings of the Thai Red Chicken Curry. The pumpkin is the only vegetable I wouldn't recommend substituting because it has as much value, if not more, than the chicken in this recipe. Freeze the leftovers or take them to work for lunch.

Wednesday

I just love this Lamb Harira! It's a mildly spiced dish that is chock full of goodness. You'll see in the recipe that celery is 'optional'. It hasn't been included in the grocery list because I can't justify the price just for this recipe. However, if you have a few stalks lying around, slice them up and throw them in with the carrot. We use both leftover meat and the bone for this stew so it will benefit from a longer cook time. I've tested it with a 1-hour simmer and it's still very full flavoured. You can also add sliced kale, silverbeet, spinach or green beans for a nutrition boost.

Thursday

In a week full of flavour bombs this Pumpkin Soup is the mildest of the recipes, but don't be fooled into thinking that it's bland. Roasting the spiced veg before it's added to the soup really makes all the difference. In saying that, this can also be made exclusively on the stovetop, by dicing up the raw pumpkin into small pieces, adding it in with the spices and increasing the simmer time to about 30 minutes. It's almost criminal not to serve this up with some type of bread to dunk into the soup!

Friday

This Chicken Lo Mein is a 30-minute meal that's as good, if not better than your local takeaway. Use any combo of veggies to bulk it up. You can also stretch this out to 6 serves pretty easily with extra noodles and veg.

Saturday

You won't usually be this spoiled for choice, but tonight you have your pick of the leftovers from this week. If you've stored them in individual servings, maybe you can let your family pick their favourite and heat it up!

Week 6 Grocery List

Ingredients in italics are Pantry Staples (page 11), so you may have them already.

Meat and Fish

- 2.5 kg bone-in leg of lamb
- 500 g boneless chicken thighs
- 300 g chicken breast

Fruit and Veg

- 7 brown onions
- 3 bulbs garlic
- 25 g fresh ginger
- 9 carrots
- 3.7 kg pumpkin – butternut, kent or jap
- 7 lemons
- 1 lime
- 1 Lebanese cucumber
- 1 kg potatoes, suitable for roasting
- 250 g eggplant
- 1 bunch coriander
- 1 bunch mint
- 2 red capsicums
- 1 zucchini
- handful of snow peas
- 400 g green beans

Fridge and Freezer

- 60 g feta
- *unsalted butter*
- 700 g *plain Greek yoghurt*

Pantry

- 1 × 114 g tin Maesri red curry paste
- 2 × 400 g tins brown lentils
- 1 × 800 g tin diced or crushed tomatoes
- 2 × 400 g tins chickpeas
- 4 × 400 g tins coconut cream
- 500 g farfalle (bowtie pasta)
- 500 g fresh egg noodles
- *extra virgin olive oil*
- *olive oil*
- *vegetable oil*
- *salt*
- *pepper*
- *paprika*
- *dried oregano*
- *ground cinnamon*
- *ground turmeric*
- *ground cumin*
- *ground coriander*
- *garlic powder*
- *dried crushed chilli flakes*
- *sesame seeds*
- *brown sugar*
- *jasmine rice*
- *light soy sauce*
- *dark soy sauce*
- *rice wine vinegar*
- *sesame oil*
- *fish sauce*
- *tomato paste*
- *vegetable, chicken and beef stock cubes/powder*
- *cornflour*

Week 6 Swap 'n' Save

Some weeks the budget is tighter than others, or you're more busy, more tired, have unexpected guests, want to mix things up, or are catering for dietary preferences. Use the tips below to make adjustments to suit.

➡ Swap out

lamb leg ⟶ 2.2–2.5 kg lamb shoulder

chicken breast ⟶ boneless chicken thigh

fresh egg noodles ⟶ 200–250 g dried egg noodles

coconut cream ⟶ coconut milk

snow peas ⟶ any green stir fry veggies

farfalle ⟶ any medium sized pasta shape

$ Pocket some savings

Lamb: Lamb roasts are often marked down at major supermarkets. Ask the staff at your local supermarket what time they usually mark down the meat and keep an eye out. A reduced leg of lamb could save you more than $10 so if you spot a bargain and you're not ready to cook this plan, freeze it!

Home brand: Buy home brand coconut cream, diced tomatoes, lentils and chickpeas for a saving of around $1 per tin.

Eggplant: If eggplant is very expensive, replace it with a couple of zucchini in the Spiced Lamb and Eggplant Farfalle. Snow peas can also be quite expensive at different times, so use green beans or even shredded cabbage in their place.

Coriander: If you don't like or can't afford fresh coriander, it can be left out altogether.

Yoghurt: The Greek yoghurt is a must for the Spiced Lamb and Eggplant Farfalle, but if you don't make the Tzatziki with the lamb, you can get away with 250 g.

Pumpkin: This powerhouse orange veg is used for both the Roasted Pumpkin Soup and the Thai Red Chicken Curry. You will need about 3.5 kg for both recipes, so this is a plan that you should cook when pumpkin is $1 to $2 per kilo. Fruit and veg shops often have great deals on whole pumpkins. I usually pick them up over the colder months for less than $1 per kilo. My preference is butternut, but kent, jap or any other variety will do.

⬜ Leftovers

If you cook this plan as written, there shouldn't be any leftover ingredients aside from the pantry staples.

Slow Cooked Greek Lamb

Tender, juicy meat that falls off the bone

SERVES 8
PREP 20 minutes
COOK 6 hours

2.5 kg leg of lamb
6 cloves garlic, smashed
2 brown onions, cut into wedges
1 tablespoon salt
1 tablespoon dried oregano
1 teaspoon paprika
1 teaspoon black pepper
½ teaspoon garlic powder
finely grated zest of 1 lemon,
    juice of 2 lemons
3 tablespoons extra virgin olive oil
1½ cups (375 ml) chicken stock

Tzatziki
1 cup (280 g) plain Greek yoghurt
1 Lebanese cucumber, grated, liquid
    strained
1 small clove garlic, crushed
2 teaspoons lemon juice
2 teaspoons extra virgin olive oil
¼ teaspoon salt
1 tablespoon finely chopped mint
    leaves

PREP

✓ Preheat the oven to 140°C. Place the lamb into a large roasting dish.

✓ Smash the garlic cloves and cut the onions into wedges.

✓ Combine the salt, oregano, paprika, black pepper, garlic powder, lemon zest and olive oil in a bowl.

✓ Cut 10–15 slits into the top of the lamb with a small sharp knife. Rub the spice mix over the top, sides and bottom of the lamb leg, ensuring that all surfaces are covered. Turn the lamb over, fat side down.

✓ Pour the chicken stock and lemon juice over the lamb then add the smashed garlic cloves and onion.

✓ Cover the lamb with 1 layer of baking paper and 1 or 2 layers of foil to ensure that it is as airtight as possible.

✓ Grate the cucumber, and strain the liquid out in a metal sieve. Combine the ingredients for the **tzatziki** in a bowl, cover and chill until ready to serve.

COOK

1. Transfer the lamb to the oven and cook for 6 hours in total.

2. About halfway through, remove from the oven. Uncover the lamb and turn it right side up. Baste the lamb with the pan juices then cover it again and return to the oven. If at any point during the cooking process, you notice that the liquid is reducing a fair bit, top it up with a little extra stock.

3. After about 5 ½ hours, check the lamb to see if it's tender and pulls away easily from the bone. If so, remove the foil and cook, uncovered, for another 15–20 minutes.

4. Remove lamb from the oven. Transfer to a serving platter or dish and cover it loosely with foil. Allow the lamb at least 15–20 minutes to rest before you serve it up.

5. If cooking the meal plan, reserve 400–450 g of meat and the bones for the **Spiced Lamb and Eggplant Farfalle** and **Lamb Harira** recipes later in the week.

6. Serve the remainder for tonight's meal, along with **Lemon Potatoes and Green Beans** and **Tzatziki**, drizzled with the pan juices.

NOTES

Dairy-free: Omit the tzatziki.

Lamb Shoulder: Lamb shoulder can be used interchangeably with the lamb leg in the oven or slow cooker.

Leftovers: Store in the fridge for up to 4 days or in the freezer for up to 3 months.

Size: If you're using a smaller or larger leg of lamb, the cook time may increase or decrease by 30–60 minutes.

Slow cooker: This is equally as succulent when cooked in the slow cooker. Follow the prep instructions to the end of step 4. Place the onions in the bottom of the slow cooker with the lamb on top then add stock, lemon juice, garlic cloves and herbs. Cover and cook on high for 5–6 hours or on low for 10–11 hours. You can crisp it up under the grill in the oven if you wish.

Greek Lemon Potatoes and Green Beans

A one-pan side with tons of flavour

SERVES 4
PREP 10 minutes
COOK 1 hour

¼ cup (60 ml) extra virgin olive oil
¼ cup (60 ml) lemon juice
2 teaspoons dried oregano
½ teaspoon garlic powder
1 teaspoon salt
1 kg potatoes, peeled and cut into thin wedges
200 g green beans, trimmed
½–¾ cup (125–180 ml) chicken or vegetable stock

To serve
2 tablespoons crumbled feta

PREP

✓ Preheat oven to 200°C.

✓ Mix the olive oil, lemon juice, oregano, garlic powder and salt in a bowl or jug.

✓ Peel the potatoes, slice them into 1 cm rounds. Wash and trim the green beans.

COOK

1. Arrange the potato wedges in a large roasting pan. Pour ¾ of the lemon oil seasoning over the potatoes and turn them to coat evenly. Set the remainder aside.

2. Pour ½ cup (125 ml) stock carefully into the corners of the tray, ensuring that it doesn't wash the lemon mixture off the potatoes.

3. Place the tray, uncovered, on a rack in the middle of the oven. Bake for 55–60 minutes in total. After 25 minutes, gently turn the potatoes with tongs and add the remaining ¼ cup (60 ml) stock if necessary.

4. At around 50 minutes, the potatoes should be light golden brown in colour and fluffy in the middle. Add the beans on top of the potatoes and drizzle the remaining lemon oil seasoning over the beans. Cook for another 8–10 minutes then remove the tray from the oven.

5. Serve up in a large shallow dish with the lemony pan juices poured over the top. Sprinkle with the crumbled feta.

NOTES

Cooking for a crowd: This recipe can be doubled, but you may need to use 2 trays (swap oven position at the halfway mark), if you'd like the potatoes to crisp up.

Dairy-free: Leave off the feta.

Leftovers: Store in the fridge for up to 3 days, reheat in the microwave.

Substitutions: Broccolini can be used in place of green beans. If cooking the potatoes without any greens, add all of the lemon oil mixture in with the potatoes at step 1.

Timing: Follow the instructions above if you're cooking as a standalone dish. If cooking in the same oven as the Greek lamb, at the lower temperature, add the potatoes to the oven 1 hour prior to the lamb being ready. When you remove the lamb to rest, crank up the heat to 200°C and cook for 10–15 minutes then add the beans and cook for another 8–10 minutes.

Spiced Lamb and Eggplant Farfalle

Oddly delicious – trust me on this one!

Eggplant
250 g eggplant, chopped into 2 cm cubes
½ teaspoon salt
2 tablespoons olive oil

Spiced lamb
1 tablespoon olive oil
1 brown onion, finely diced
2 cloves garlic, crushed
200–250 g leftover Slow Cooked Greek Lamb (page 126), chopped
1 teaspoon ground cumin
½ teaspoon salt
½ teaspoon dried chilli flakes
3 tablespoons chopped mint leaves

Yoghurt sauce
1 cup (280 g) plain Greek yoghurt
1 large clove garlic
½ teaspoon ground cumin
¼ teaspoon salt
squeeze of lemon juice

Pasta
500 g farfalle
1 tablespoon unsalted butter

To serve
3 tablespoons chopped fresh mint leaves
2 tablespoons crumbled feta
½ lemon, sliced into thin wedges

PREP

✓ Preheat the oven to 220°C. Line a large baking tray with baking paper.

✓ Bring a large pot of salted water to the boil on the stove.

✓ Chop the eggplant into 2cm cubes. Sprinkle with salt, drizzle with oil and spread out on the baking tray.

✓ For the spiced lamb, dice the onion and crush the garlic. Chop the lamb into small pieces.

✓ To make the yoghurt sauce, mix yoghurt, garlic, cumin and salt together in a bowl. Cut the lemon half into 6 wedges and squeeze 1 wedge into the yoghurt sauce. Set aside.

COOK

1. Put the tray of eggplant into the oven and bake for about 15 minutes or until lightly browned and starting to crisp.

2. Once the water is boiling, add the pasta and cook according to packet directions, until al dente.

3. Meanwhile, to cook the lamb, heat the oil in a large frying pan over medium heat. Add the onion and cook, stirring, for a few minutes until soft. Add the garlic, cook for another minute then add the lamb, cumin, salt and chilli flakes. Cook, stirring, for a few minutes then add the chopped mint and the eggplant. Turn off the heat.

4. The pasta should now be ready. Drain in a colander, then return to the pot. Add butter and stir through until melted.

5. Divide pasta among bowls. Top with lamb and eggplant mixture and yoghurt sauce. Sprinkle with mint, crumbled feta and serve with a lemon wedge.

NOTES

Credit: This recipe has been adapted from a recipe titled **Pasta with Turkish-Style Lamb, Eggplant and Yogurt Sauce**, created by Melissa Clark and published in the *New York Times*.

Gluten-free: Use gluten-free pasta.

Vegetables: Use 200–250 g of zucchini instead of eggplant. It doesn't need to be roasted, just sauté some thinly sliced zucchini for a couple of minutes with the garlic and onion.

Lamb: If you don't have leftover roast lamb meat, you can use 250 g lamb mince. Brown the mince after the onion is cooked at step 3, then add the garlic and spices.

Leftovers: Because we're reheating cooked meat for the second time, it's essential that leftovers are stored correctly and that it's reheated safely in the microwave to a high temperature (75°C). Store in the fridge for 24 hours. I don't recommend freezing this dish.

Thai Red Chicken Curry

My favourite Thai curry with plenty of veg

SERVES 8
PREP 15 minutes
COOK 30 minutes

4 cloves garlic, crushed
1 tablespoon finely grated fresh ginger
700 g pumpkin
2 large carrots, sliced
1 zucchini, halved lengthways then
   sliced
1 red capsicum, sliced
200 g green beans, halved
2 tablespoons finely chopped
   coriander stems (optional)
500 g chicken thigh fillets, trimmed,
   thinly sliced
1 tablespoon vegetable oil
114 g tin Maesri red curry paste
3 × 400 ml tins coconut cream
2 tablespoons brown sugar
1 tablespoon fish sauce
1 tablespoon lime juice

To serve
steamed jasmine rice
coriander leaves
chilli, diced
lime slices or wedges

PREP

✓ Crush the garlic and grate the ginger. Peel the pumpkin and chop into 2–3 cm cubes, peel and slice the carrots into 1 cm rounds. Slice the zucchini and capsicum, trim and halve the green beans. Finely chop the coriander stems.

✓ Trim the fat from the chicken thighs and thinly slice.

COOK

1. Heat the oil in a large frying pan, wok or pot over medium-high heat then add the curry paste, garlic and ginger. Stir for 2 minutes.

2. Add half a tin of coconut cream to the paste mixture and cook while stirring for about 2 minutes or until the liquid has reduced by about a third.

3. Pour in the remaining coconut cream then add the sugar, fish sauce, lime juice and chopped coriander stems (if using). Bring just to the boil.

4. Stir in the pumpkin, carrot and chicken. Reduce heat to medium-low and simmer, partially covered, for about 15 minutes or until the pumpkin is tender.

5. Add zucchini, beans and capsicum. Cook for another 5 minutes or until vegetables are cooked to your liking. Taste to check spice level. Add more coconut cream for a milder curry. Add a little more lime juice, sugar or fish sauce to balance the flavour if needed.

6. Serve with steamed rice, and add coriander leaves, chilli and lime slices or wedges.

WEEK 6

NOTES

Balancing flavours: If it tastes a little acidic or sour, add more brown sugar. If you'd like a saltier flavour, add fish sauce. For a fresher flavour, add another squeeze of lime juice.

Leftovers: Store in the fridge for 3 days, freeze for 1 month. Reheat in the microwave or on the stovetop. Freeze any leftover curry paste for up to 1 month.

Spice: Cook the recipe as written for a medium-hot curry. If you prefer a milder curry, start with half of the Maesri tin (about 3 tablespoons). If you find yourself with a curry that's way too hot, you can add chicken stock or additional coconut cream. If you're cooking from the meal plan you'll have half a tin spare as you only need 200 ml for the Roasted Pumpkin Soup.

Substitutions: Coconut milk can be used in place of the coconut cream. Choose seasonal vegetables in place of those listed in the recipe.

Lamb Harira

A nourishing Moroccan stew infused with so much flavour

SERVES 8
PREP 15 minutes
COOK 2 hours

1 large brown onion, diced
3 carrots, peeled and diced
4 cloves garlic, crushed
2 tablespoons finely chopped
    coriander stems and leaves
2 teaspoons ground cumin
1½ teaspoons ground turmeric
1½ teaspoons ground cinnamon
1 teaspoon paprika
½ teaspoon salt
200–250 g leftover Slow Cooked
    Greek Lamb (page 126),
    chopped, plus the bones
2 tablespoons olive oil
2 tablespoons tomato paste
800 g tin diced or crushed tomatoes
2 × 400 g tins brown lentils,
    rinsed and drained
2 × 400 g tins chickpeas,
    rinsed and drained
5 cups (1.25 litres) beef stock
juice of 1 lemon

To serve
coriander leaves
plain Greek yoghurt
couscous or steamed basmati rice
    (optional)

PREP

✓ Dice the onion, peel and dice the carrots and crush the garlic. Finely chop the coriander leaves and stems.

✓ Add the cumin, turmeric, cinnamon, paprika and salt to a small bowl and mix.

✓ Chop the lamb into small pieces.

COOK

1. Heat the oil in a large frying pan or pot over medium heat.

2. Add the onion and carrot and cook, stirring, for 3–4 minutes, until starting to soften.

3. Add the garlic and stir for a minute then add the chopped lamb, tomato paste and combined spices. Stir for a minute or two then add the crushed tomatoes.

4. Add in the lamb bones with the coriander stems and leaves and pour over 4 cups (1 litre) beef stock.

5. Bring the soup to a simmer then reduce heat to low. Cover and cook for 1–2 hours. The longer it cooks, the more the flavour will develop.

6. Add the lentils and chickpeas and cook, uncovered, on low for another 20 minutes. Remove the bones.

7. Season with salt and pepper (to taste) and cook for another 10 minutes.

8. Serve topped with coriander leaves and a swirl of Greek yoghurt. To stretch it further, serve over rice or couscous.

NOTES

Dietaries: For dairy-free, leave off the yoghurt. For gluten-free, serve with rice rather than couscous, if using.

Lamb: This can also be made using lamb offcuts or any cut of lamb that is suitable for stewing. The lamb should be browned prior to step 1 then removed and added back in at step 4. The cook time should be increased to 3–4 hours on the stove or in the oven at 150°C.

Leftovers: Because we're reheating cooked meat for the second time, it's essential that leftovers are stored correctly and that it's reheated safely in the microwave to a high temperature (75°C). Store in the fridge for 1 day, freeze for up to 3 months.

Spice: This dish is quite mild and even though I'm a spice fiend, I love it just like this. If you cook it and you're feeling like it could do with more flavour, add an extra ½ teaspoon of the cumin, paprika, cinnamon and turmeric the next time you make it.

Roasted Pumpkin Soup

Creamy and gently spiced

SERVES 8
PREP 10 minutes
COOK 40 minutes

2 brown onions, diced
6 cloves garlic, crushed
3 large carrots, peeled
    and thickly sliced
3 kg pumpkin (unpeeled weight),
    peeled and cut into 4 cm pieces.
3 tablespoons olive oil
½ teaspoon ground cumin
½ teaspoon ground cinnamon
¼ teaspoon pepper
1 teaspoon salt
8 cups (2 litres) chicken or
    vegetable stock
200 ml (½ tin) coconut cream

To serve
crusty bread or garlic bread (optional)
coriander leaves (optional)

PREP

✓ Preheat the oven to 190°C. Line a large baking tray with baking paper.

✓ Dice the onion and crush the garlic. Peel the carrots and thickly slice.

✓ Peel the pumpkin and chop into 4 cm pieces.

COOK

1. Arrange pumpkin and carrot evenly on the baking tray. Drizzle with 2 tablespoons olive oil, then sprinkle with cumin, cinnamon, pepper and ½ teaspoon of the salt.

2. Roast for about 30 minutes, or until soft (enjoy the beautiful scent!).

3. About 10 minutes before the pumpkin and carrot are ready, heat remaining olive oil in a large pot over medium heat. Cook onions for 5 minutes, stirring occasionally, then add garlic and the other ½ teaspoon salt. Cook for another couple of minutes, until soft.

4. Remove the vegetables from the oven. Tip them carefully into the pot, stir for a minute then add 1.5 litres stock. Bring to the boil then reduce heat to low. Simmer, covered, for 15 minutes or until vegetables are very soft.

5. Turn off heat and blend soup with a stick blender, adding more stock for a thinner consistency. Check seasoning and add salt or pepper to taste, then put it back on low heat for another few minutes.

6. Serve with a swirl of coconut cream, a sprinkle of coriander leaves (if using) in each bowl and a large hunk of crusty bread or garlic bread, if you like.

NOTES

Gluten-free: Serve with gluten-free bread, if using.

Leftovers: Store in the fridge for 4 days or in the freezer for 3 months. Reheat in the microwave or on the stovetop.

Pumpkin: Either jap, kent or butternut can be used for this recipe.

Spices: Try seasoning the pumpkin with different combinations of spices, such as cinnamon/nutmeg or cumin/coriander/turmeric.

Chicken Lo Mein

Simple but flavourful Chinese stir-fry

Chicken marinade
300 g chicken breast fillet, sliced thinly
1 tablespoon light soy sauce
2 teaspoons cornflour
1 teaspoon sesame oil

Sauce
2 tablespoons dark soy sauce
2 tablespoons light soy sauce
1 teaspoon rice wine vinegar
1 teaspoon brown sugar
¼ teaspoon ground black pepper
1 teaspoon sesame oil
1 tablespoon cornflour
¼ cup (60 ml) chicken stock or water

Stir-fry
4 cloves garlic, crushed
1 brown onion, finely sliced or diced
1 red capsicum, sliced
1 large carrot, peeled and thinly sliced
handful of snow peas or
    sugar snap peas
500 g fresh egg noodles
    (or 250–300 g dried noodles)
2 tablespoons vegetable oil

To serve
sesame seeds
sliced green onions

PREP

✓ For the **chicken marinade**, thinly slice the chicken and add to a bowl with marinade ingredients, mix to coat well and set aside.

✓ Mix **sauce** ingredients together in a bowl or jug.

✓ To prep the **stir-fry** component, crush the garlic and finely slice or dice the onion. Slice the capsicum, peel and thinly slice the carrot, trim the snow peas.

✓ Put fresh noodles into a colander and rinse with hot water. If using dried egg noodles, prepare according to packet instructions.

COOK

1. Heat a wok or large frying pan over high heat then add 1 tablespoon oil.

2. When oil is hot, stir-fry the chicken for a few minutes, until cooked through. Transfer to a plate.

3. Bring the wok back up to high heat then heat remaining oil. Add the onion, stir-fry for a minute then add the garlic. Add the carrot, capsicum and snow peas. Stir-fry for another minute.

4. Add the noodles, sauce and chicken to the wok. Stir well to combine and cook for a couple more minutes to heat through.

5. Serve into bowls, and top with sliced green onions and sesame seeds.

NOTES

Leftovers: Store in the fridge for 2 days and reheat in the microwave or a wok. I don't recommend freezing this dish.

Noodles: You can purchase any egg noodles from the fridge or the shelves at your local supermarket. I like to use fresh lo mein or chow mein noodles. You can also use cooked spaghetti for this dish as a substitute.

Vegetables: Use any stir-fry vegetables for this dish. You can substitute the listed ingredients with cheaper seasonal options if you prefer. I'd aim for around 3 cups of vegetables for 4 servings.

WEEK 7

Double or Nothing

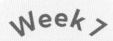

Week 7

Sunday
Twin Roast Chickens

Monday
Vietnamese Noodle Salad

Tuesday
Chicken Taco Soup

Wednesday
Korean Beef Bowls

Thursday
Beef and Lentil Bolognese

Friday
Thai Green Fish Curry

Saturday
Beef and Lentil Bolognese

Week 7 at a Glance

 **Servings: 28**
plus 7 leftovers

 $2.47
per serve

Put in a bit of extra effort on the first night of this plan with the **Twin Roast Chickens** and you'll find that the rest of the week's dinner prep is fairly relaxed. If you're going to roast one bird, why not throw another one in? You'll have enough meat for at least two more recipes and if you're lucky, you might even have some left over for a chicken sandwich or two!

Sunday

We start this week with the **Twin Roast Chickens**. One will be served tonight with the **Ultra Crispy Roast Potatoes**, **Glazed Carrots** and **Roast Chicken Gravy**. I like to allow about 2 hours from the very start of prep until all of the components are served up on the plate. Read the recipe notes for tips on timing each recipe. Once cooked, shred the meat from the second chicken and pop it in the fridge. You'll use half for the **Vietnamese Noodle Salad** and the remainder for Tuesday's **Chicken Taco Soup**.

Monday

This **Vietnamese Noodle Salad** is bursting with colour, freshness and flavour. You'll make enough for about 6 servings. I love taking this to work for lunch or sending it in the kids' lunchboxes. Just keep the dressing separate in a small leak-proof container. To elevate the dish and add another textural element (for serving at home – not school), you can add ¼ cup finely chopped peanuts as garnish.

Tuesday

This **Chicken Taco Soup** is my son Seth's favourite meal from this week's plan. It's a light summery soup that tastes even better the next day. It makes about 8 serves so you can either freeze or reheat the leftovers. I'm quite happy to eat this on its own as a light meal but if you want to add some extra carbs, it pairs perfectly with **Cornbread Muffins** (recipe in Week 1, page 23) or tortilla chips.

Wednesday

If you're looking for just one recipe to try from this week's plan I'd recommend these **Korean Beef Bowls**. It's such a quick, cheap meal to put together and the flavours are bold but still very child-friendly. The addition of the fried egg is a must if you're cooking for teenagers or bigger eaters. To bulk it up further you could also serve up steamed Asian greens or stir fry some grated carrot or zucchini with the beef.

Thursday

We're keeping it simple and familiar with tonight's **Beef and Lentil Bolognese**. Almost everyone has their own bolognese recipe so I'm going to leave it up to you to decide whether you want to follow my recipe or use the base ingredients to develop your own beef and lentil version. You will have enough sauce for two nights but this freezes beautifully so pop it in the freezer if you already have Saturday night's dinner covered.

Friday

This week's Friday Night Fakeaway is the **Thai Green Fish Curry**. I know that not everyone is keen on fish so I've given you instructions in the recipe notes to substitute it with chicken. This is one of my favourite curries but beware . . . the Maesri green curry paste is far spicier than the red variety or the massaman. Do not under any circumstances add the entire tin if you don't tolerate spice well!

Saturday

If you've had a big day and don't feel like cooking, you'll be thankful to have the **Beef and Lentil Bolognese** in the fridge to heat up for dinner. It might sound a bit odd but whenever I serve up a particular pasta sauce 2 nights in one week, I like to use different pasta shapes. My favourites are rigatoni and linguine – it almost makes it feel like a different dish and not 'leftovers'.

Week 7 Grocery List

Ingredients in italics are Pantry Staples (page 11), so you may have them already.

Meat and Fish

- 2 × 1.5–2 kg whole chickens
- 1 kg beef mince
- 500 g white fish fillets

Fruit and Veg

- 3 brown onions
- 3 bulbs garlic
- 25 g fresh ginger
- 2.5 kg carrots
- 1 lemon
- 5 limes
- 1 kg potatoes, suitable for roasting
- 1 bunch coriander
- 1 bunch mint
- 1 large red capsicum
- 1 large continental cucumber
- 2 zucchini
- 200 g green beans
- ½ wombok (Chinese cabbage)
- 1 bunch green onions

Fridge and Freezer

- *unsalted butter*
- 4 *eggs*
- *parmesan*

Pantry

- 1 × 114 g tin Maesri green curry paste
- 1 × 400 g tin brown lentils
- 1 × 400 g tin black beans
- 1 × 400 g tin corn kernels
- 1 × 400 g tin diced or crushed tomatoes
- 2 × 800 g tins diced or crushed tomatoes
- 3 × 400 g tins coconut cream
- 2 × 500 g packs pasta
- 200 g vermicelli rice noodles
- *olive oil*
- *vegetable oil*
- *salt*
- *pepper*
- *paprika*
- *dried oregano*
- *garlic powder*
- *ground cumin*
- *cayenne pepper*
- *dried chilli flakes*
- *brown sugar*
- *caster sugar*
- *jasmine rice*
- *light soy sauce*
- *dark soy sauce*
- *sesame oil*
- *rice wine vinegar*
- *fish sauce*
- *sriracha*
- *tomato paste*
- *mayonnaise*
- *chicken stock cubes/powder*
- *beef stock cubes/powder*
- *cornflour*
- *plain flour*
- *sesame seeds*

Week 7 Swap 'n' Save

➡️ Swap out

beef mince $\longrightarrow$ pork mince

fish fillets $\longrightarrow$ chicken breast or thigh

1 continental cucumber $\longrightarrow$ 2–3 Lebanese cucumbers

tinned black beans $\longrightarrow$ tinned kidney beans

tinned corn kernels $\longrightarrow$ frozen corn kernels

💲 Pocket some savings

Chicken: The price of a whole chicken varies greatly between brands and stores by about $3 per kg which makes quite a difference when you're purchasing 2 of them. Look for prices around $5 per kg or less at your local supermarket or butcher.

Mince: Beef mince is always cheaper at the supermarket if you buy the 1 kg packs rather than 2 × 500 g packs.

Green onions: The green onions are a substantial ingredient in the **Vietnamese Noodle Salad** but an optional garnish only in two other recipes this week. You could leave off the garnish and replace them with a small, finely sliced red onion in the noodle salad to save a couple of dollars.

Coriander: You can leave out the coriander in this week's meal plan if you don't love it or can't afford it. Increase the mint to 1 cup in the **Vietnamese Noodle Salad** as a substitute and if you have any flat leaf parsley, you can garnish the **Chicken Taco Soup** with that instead.

⭐ Splurge

If you're in a position to treat yourself this week, the following will add some extra deliciousness to your meals.

- **Garlic Bread** (page 24): to serve with the **Beef and Lentil Bolognese**
- **Cornbread Muffins** (page 23): to serve with the **Chicken Taco Soup**

🥡 Leftovers

You'll likely have some mint left over this week. This is great to use to make **Tzatziki** (page 173) or **keftedes mixture** (page 170).

Twin Roast Chickens

Twice the reward for minimal effort

SERVES 4–5 PER CHICKEN
PREP 20 minutes
COOK 70–80 minutes

2 × 1.5–2 kg whole chickens
squeezed lemon halves
    (from the wet mix)
4 cloves garlic, smashed
1 brown onion, halved

Wet mix
3 tablespoons unsalted butter, melted
juice of 1 lemon
2 tablespoons olive oil

Dry mix
2 teaspoons salt
½ teaspoon garlic powder
½ teaspoon ground black pepper

PREP

✓ Preheat the oven to 220°C.

✓ Remove chickens from the fridge and place them, breast side up, side-by-side in a large baking dish or roasting pan.

✓ Melt the butter for the **wet mix**, juice the lemon then combine the ingredients in a small bowl and set aside. For the **dry mix**, combine the ingredients in a separate bowl.

✓ Spread about half of the wet mix onto the skin of both birds (don't forget underneath). Pour 1 tablespoon into each of the cavities and massage 1 tablespoon in between the skin and the breast of each bird.

✓ Sprinkle 1 teaspoon of the dry mix over the skin of each chicken and spread it gently with your fingertips, pour ½ teaspoon into each cavity and then massage any that remains under the breast skin.

✓ Stuff each chicken cavity with a squeezed lemon half, 2 smashed garlic cloves and half a brown onion.

✓ With the chicken breast side up, fold the wings underneath to prevent them burning. Using kitchen string, tie the ends of the legs (drumsticks) together.

COOK

1. Put the baking dish on a rack in the middle of the oven and cook for 15 minutes. Use this time to start on your vegetables/sides.

2. Reduce the heat to 200°C. Roast chickens for a further 50 minutes, then remove from the oven to check if they are done. (The chicken is ready when you prick the thigh with skewer and its juices run clear, or when its internal temperature reaches 75°C when tested with a meat thermometer. If in doubt, cut a piece to check it's completely cooked through and not still pink in the middle.) If it's not yet ready pop it back in and check every 10 minutes.

3. If the skin is not as brown as you'd like, put the grill on and brown the chickens for a few minutes.

4. When ready, remove the baking dish from the oven. Transfer the chickens to a platter or serving dish, tipping the cavity juices into the baking dish. Set aside to use in the **Roast Chicken Gravy** (page 153). Cover the chickens loosely with foil and let them rest for 10–15 minutes before serving.

NOTES

Dairy-free: Omit the butter in the wet mix and increase the oil to 5 tablespoons.

Leftovers: Leftover cooked chicken meat can be stored in the fridge for up to 3 days or frozen for up to 2 months. Keep the chicken frames and use them to make homemade chicken stock.

Meal Plan: If you're following the meal plan, serve up one of the birds plus the wings of the second bird for dinner. Shred the rest of the meat from the second bird and store it in a container in the fridge for your next two meals.

Ultra Crispy Roast Potatoes

The most incredible roast potatoes you've ever made

2 tablespoons salt
1–1.5 kg potatoes, peeled
    and cut into 5 cm chunks
2 tablespoons unsalted butter
2 tablespoons olive oil
3 whole garlic cloves, smashed
    (optional)

PREP

✓ Preheat the oven to 200°C .

✓ Put a large pot of salted water on to boil.

✓ Smash the garlic cloves with the side of a large knife then add them to a large roasting tray with the butter and oil. Set aside.

✓ Peel the potatoes and cut them into 5 cm chunks.

COOK

1. Add the potatoes to the pot of salted water and bring it to the boil over high heat. Once the water is boiling, reduce the heat to medium-low and cook them for another 10 minutes or until they're fork tender, but not falling apart.

2. Just before the potatoes are ready, pop the roasting tray into the oven for a few minutes to melt the butter and heat the oil.

3. Meanwhile, drain the potatoes in a large colander. Shake the colander to jostle the potatoes around so that they're roughed up a bit. Season them well with salt and pepper.

4. Remove the tray from the oven then carefully arrange the potatoes on the tray, spread slightly apart.

5. Roast for 25 minutes then remove tray from oven, turn each potato and bake for another 20–25 minutes, until nicely browned and super crispy. Remove from the oven and season again with salt and pepper.

WEEK 7

NOTES

Timing: When I cook these with the **Twin Roast Chickens**, I start to prepare them as soon as the chicken goes in the oven. I then add the potatoes about 15 minutes after I turn the oven down to 200°C. They roast for about 35–40 minutes with the chicken, and another 10–15 minutes while the chicken is resting.

Potatoes: I usually buy brushed potatoes for this recipe as they're often cheapest but you can use any variety that is suitable for roasting such as Dutch cream, coliban or desiree. 1 kg is plenty for 4 servings but my family inhale these, so I'll often roast 1.5 kg to ensure that everyone has their fill!

Glazed Carrots

Sweet, savoury, delicious

SERVES 4–5
PREP 10 minutes
COOK 25 minutes

1 kg carrots, peeled, cut diagonally
  into 3 cm chunks
4 tablespoons unsalted butter
1 tablespoon olive oil
3 tablespoons brown sugar or honey
1 clove garlic, crushed
¼ teaspoon salt

PREP

- ✓ Preheat the oven to 200°C. Line a baking tray with baking paper and bring a medium pot of generously salted water to the boil.
- ✓ Peel the carrots and cut diagonally into 3 cm chunks.

COOK

1. Start by steaming or boiling the carrots (up to you). If steaming, cook for 10–15 minutes. If boiling, cook for 5 minutes or until fork-tender. Drain and transfer to a bowl.

2. Drain any remaining water from the pan and reduce the heat to low. Add the butter, oil, sugar (or honey) garlic and salt. When the butter has melted and the glaze is a smooth consistency, return the carrots to the pan and gently stir to coat with the glaze.

3. Transfer to a baking tray and roast for about 10 minutes or until they're slightly caramelised. Remove from the oven and season with salt and freshly ground black pepper.

NOTES

Timing: When I cook these with the **Twin Roast Chickens** and **Ultra Crispy Roast Potatoes**, I start my prep and cook the carrots after the potatoes are in the oven. I then roast the carrots while the chicken is resting.

Stovetop method: If oven space is scarce, these can be made on the stovetop. Once coated with the glaze in step 2, cook, stirring, on low heat for a few minutes more.

Roast Chicken Gravy

A Sunday roast essential

SERVES 4–5
PREP/COOK 15 minutes

reserved pan juices in baking pan
(**from Twin Roast Chickens**, page 146)
3 tablespoons plain flour
¼ teaspoon ground black or white
pepper
1 cup (250 ml) chicken stock,
plus more if needed

STEPS

1. Scrape all of the leftover meat, juices and fat off the bottom of the baking dish and tip them into a measuring jug or medium bowl. Let it sit for a couple of minutes. The fat will rise to the top and you can use a spoon to skim off as much of it as you can.

2. Measure out ½ cup of the remaining drippings and tip into a small saucepan or frying pan. Place over medium-low heat.

3. Add the flour to the pan with the pepper. Stir the flour and drippings together to make a paste (roux) and continue stirring until it begins to brown.

4. Slowly pour the stock in while stirring or whisking continuously. Raise the heat to medium and bring the gravy to a simmer. Keep stirring for a couple of minutes or until the gravy thickens.

5. Taste and season with salt and pepper. Strain through a sieve if you want a perfectly smooth texture.

NOTES

Consistency: If the gravy is far too thick, just add more stock. If it's not thickening at all after simmering for 5 minutes, mix 1 tablespoon of cornflour with 1 tablespoon of water in a small bowl to make a cornflour slurry, then whisk into the gravy to thicken.

Leftovers: Store in the fridge for up to 4 days. Freeze for up to 3 months. Reheat on the stovetop, adding a little extra stock if needed.

Timing: Make the gravy while the chicken is resting.

Vietnamese Noodle Salad

An explosion of summery freshness

SERVES 6

PREP 20 minutes

Dressing

5 tablespoons caster sugar
¼ cup (60 ml) fish sauce
2 tablespoons rice wine vinegar
finely grated zest and juice of 1 lime
2 cloves garlic
½–1 teaspoon sriracha

Salad

200 g vermicelli rice noodles
½ wombok (Chinese cabbage),
   finely sliced
¾ cup mint leaves, roughly chopped
½ cup coriander leaves, roughly
   chopped
2 large carrots, coarsely grated or
   cut into matchsticks
½ large continental cucumbers,
   thinly sliced or cut into matchsticks
½ large red capsicum, thinly sliced
2 green onions, thinly sliced
2 cups (320 g) shredded
   Roast Chicken (page 146)

To serve

mint leaves
coriander leaves
lime wedges

STEPS

1. Place noodles in a large, heatproof bowl and cover with boiling water. Set aside and allow noodles to soften for 7–10 minutes.

2. Combine **dressing** ingredients with 3 tablespoons water in a medium bowl or jug. Stir together well until the sugar dissolves.

3. To make the **salad**, finely slice the wombok, roughly chop the mint and coriander, grate the carrot, slice the cucumber, capsicum and green onions. Add to your largest salad bowl, one at a time. Add the chicken and toss gently to combine.

4. Once the noodles are soft, drain them into a colander and rinse under cold running water until cool. Give them a bit of a squeeze to remove as much water as possible. Add the noodles to the salad and toss until evenly combined.

5. Divide among bowls, top with fresh herbs and serve with lime wedges. Allow each person to dress their own salad at the table according to their taste.

NOTES

Chicken: If you want to make this as a meal without roasting a chicken, pan-fry 300–500 g chicken thigh fillets. Thinly slice and use in place of the shredded chicken.

Leftovers: Store for up to 2 days in the fridge (undressed).

Shortcut: If you don't want to make your own dressing or you're looking for a milder alternative, the Pandaroo Vietnamese salad dressing sold in the major supermarkets is very tasty.

Chicken Taco Soup

Light, but satisfying

SERVES 8
PREP 15 minutes
COOK 25 minutes

1 large brown onion, diced
½ large red capsicum, diced
4 carrots, peeled and diced
4 cloves garlic, crushed
2 tablespoons finely chopped
   coriander stems
2 teaspoons paprika
2 teaspoons ground cumin
¼ teaspoon cayenne pepper
1 teaspoon salt
1 tablespoon olive oil
8 cups (2 litres) chicken stock
400 g tin diced or crushed tomatoes
2 cups (320 g) shredded
   Roast Chicken (page 146)
400 g tin black beans,
   rinsed and drained
400 g tin corn kernels,
   rinsed and drained
juice of 1 lime

To serve
coriander leaves
green onions, sliced
lime wedges

PREP

✓ Dice the onion and capsicum. Peel and dice the carrots.

✓ Crush the garlic and finely chop the coriander stems.

✓ Combine the paprika, cumin, cayenne pepper and salt in a small bowl.

COOK

1. Heat oil in a large pot over medium heat. Add the onion and cook, stirring, for 4 minutes. Add the capsicum and carrot and cook for another 3 minutes. Stir in the garlic and spice mixture and cook, stirring, for a minute.

2. Add the coriander stems, chicken stock, diced tomatoes, chicken, black beans and corn kernels to the pot and bring to a gentle simmer.

3. Reduce heat to low and cook, uncovered, for as little as 10 minutes or up to 30 minutes for a deeper flavour (partially cover after 10 minutes).

4. Just before serving, stir in the lime juice then taste and season with salt and pepper.

5. Ladle into bowls and top with coriander leaves and green onions. Serve with lime wedges.

WEEK 7

NOTES

Spice: If you want a really spicy soup, add ½–¾ teaspoon cayenne pepper. Alternatively, if you're concerned about it being too hot, you can omit it or just add a tiny pinch.

Substitutions: If you don't like coriander, replace the garnish with parsley or leave it out altogether. Kidney beans can be used instead of black beans.

Sides: I often serve this soup with **Cornbread Muffins** (page 23) or tortilla chips.

Leftovers: Because we're reheating cooked chicken for the second time, it's essential that leftovers are stored correctly and it's reheated safely in the microwave to a high temperature (75°C). Store in the fridge for 24 hours, freeze for up to 3 months.

Korean Beef Bowls

A family-friendly flavour bomb in under 30 minutes

Sauce
3 tablespoons light soy sauce
1 tablespoon dark soy sauce
3–4 tablespoons brown sugar
1 teaspoon sesame oil
½–1 teaspoon sriracha

Stir-fry
1 tablespoon vegetable oil
3 cloves garlic, crushed
1 tablespoon finely grated fresh ginger
500 g beef mince

Sriracha mayo
¼ cup (75 g) mayonnaise
1–2 teaspoons sriracha, to taste

To serve
steamed jasmine rice
½ continental cucumber, thinly sliced
1 large carrot, grated or cut into
    matchsticks
green onions, sliced
sesame seeds
4 fried eggs
dried chilli flakes

PREP

✓ Start cooking the rice.

✓ Combine the **sauce** ingredients in a bowl or jug. Mix and set aside.

✓ Crush the garlic and grate the ginger. Slice the cucumber and grate or slice the carrot into matchsticks.

✓ Make the **sriracha mayo** (if not buying premade).

COOK

1. Heat a wok or large frying pan over high heat then add the oil.

2. When oil is hot, stir-fry the garlic and ginger for 10 seconds. Add the beef mince and cook for 5–7 minutes, breaking it up as it cooks, until mostly browned. Meanwhile, fry the eggs in a separate pan.

3. Give the **sauce** a quick stir and pour it into the pan. Stir to coat the beef and stir-fry for another couple of minutes. Taste and adjust the spice and sugar levels as desired.

4. Divide among bowls with the steamed rice, cucumber and carrot. Top with sliced green onions, sesame seeds and a fried egg, then sprinkle with chilli flakes. Drizzle the sriracha mayo over the top or serve on the side.

NOTES

Gluten-free: Replace the light and dark soy sauces with 4 tablespoons tamari or gluten-free soy sauce.

Leftovers: Store leftovers in the fridge for 3 days. Reheat beef and rice in the microwave. This dish is best eaten fresh.

Sriracha mayo: The ratio I use when making sriracha mayo is about 1 part sriracha to 5 parts mayonnaise. If you're cautious with spice, start by adding ½ teaspoon, then taste and add more if you can handle it! To elevate it further, you can add a pinch of salt and a tiny squeeze of lemon or lime juice.

Substitutions: If you don't have dark soy sauce you can add an extra tablespoon of light. Steamed broccoli, broccolini or any other greens are a great substitute for the cucumber and carrot. Pork mince can be used instead of beef. A side of kimchi takes it up another notch.

Beef and Lentil Bolognese

A chunky, veg-filled twist on a classic

1 large brown onion, diced
3 carrots, peeled and diced
1 zucchini, grated
4 cloves garlic, crushed
2 tablespoons olive oil
500 g beef mince
1 teaspoon salt
3 tablespoons tomato paste
1 tablespoon dried oregano
1 teaspoon dried chilli flakes
2 beef stock cubes, crumbled
1 teaspoon caster sugar
2 × 800 g tins diced or crushed
    tomatoes
400 g tin brown lentils,
    rinsed and drained

To serve
500 g pasta
finely grated or shaved parmesan
garlic bread (optional)

PREP

✓ Dice the onion, peel and dice the carrots, grate the zucchini and crush the garlic.

COOK

1. Heat the oil in a large frying pan or pot over medium heat.

2. Add the onion and carrot and cook for 4–5 minutes, stirring occasionally, until soft.

3. Add the garlic, cook for 1 minute then turn the heat up to medium-high. Add the beef mince and salt and cook for about 5 minutes, breaking it up as it cooks, until browned.

4. Add tomato paste, oregano and chilli flakes and stir through for 1–2 minutes, then stir in the stock cubes, sugar and tinned tomatoes. Bring sauce to a simmer, then add grated zucchini and reduce heat to low.

5. Let sauce simmer, uncovered, for 15 minutes. Start boiling the water for the pasta once the sauce starts simmering so it's ready at about the same time.

6. Add the lentils to the sauce and simmer for another few minutes. If the sauce is too thick, add ½ cup water. Taste and season well with salt and freshly ground black pepper.

7. Serve over pasta, with grated or shaved parmesan, and garlic bread on the side (if using).

WEEK 7

NOTES

Beef: I recommend 3 or 4-star beef mince for this recipe. You can also replace the beef mince with pork mince or a pork and veal mince mixture.

Dietaries: For gluten-free, use gluten-free pasta. For dairy-free omit the parmesan.

Leftovers: Store in the fridge for up to 4 days and freeze for up to 3 months. Reheat in the microwave or on the stovetop.

Seasoning: Replace the oregano and chilli flakes with 1½ tablespoons Italian mixed herbs.

Thai Green Fish Curry

An aromatic fakeaway with a spicy kick

SERVES 4–5
PREP 10 minutes
COOK 20 minutes

3 cloves garlic, crushed
1 tablespoon finely grated fresh ginger
1 zucchini, halved lengthways, sliced
200 g green beans, trimmed
1 tablespoon finely chopped
    coriander stems
500 g white fish fillets
2 tablespoons vegetable oil
3 tablespoons Maesri green curry paste
3 × 400 ml tins coconut cream
1 tablespoon fish sauce
1 tablespoon lime juice
1 tablespoon brown sugar

To serve
steamed jasmine rice
coriander leaves
lime wedges

PREP

✓ Start cooking the rice.

✓ Crush the garlic and grate the ginger.

✓ Halve the zucchini lengthways and slice. Trim the green beans. Finely chop the coriander stems.

✓ Slice each fish fillet into 4 pieces.

COOK

1. Heat the oil in a large frying pan, wok or pot over medium-high heat then add the curry paste, garlic and ginger. Cook, stirring, for 2 minutes.

2. Add ½ tin coconut cream to the paste mixture and cook, stirring, for about 2 minutes or until the liquid has reduced by about a third.

3. Pour in the remaining 2 ½ tins coconut cream, add the fish sauce, lime juice, sugar and chopped coriander stems (if using) and bring to a gentle boil.

4. Add the fish, zucchini and beans and cook for another 7–8 minutes or until the vegetables are cooked and the fish is opaque. Taste to check spice level and flavours. Add a little more lime juice, sugar or fish sauce to balance flavour if required.

5. Divide among bowls with steamed rice. Top with coriander leaves and serve with lime wedges.

NOTES

Balancing flavours: If it tastes a little acidic or sour, add more brown sugar. If you'd like a saltier flavour, add fish sauce. For a fresher flavour, add another squeeze of lime juice.

Fish: I use thawed frozen basa or barramundi which can be bought at the seafood counter of major supermarkets. You could also purchase frozen fish and thaw it yourself.

Leftovers: Store in the fridge for 3 days, freeze for 1 month. Reheat in the microwave or on the stovetop. Freeze any leftover curry paste for up to 1 month.

Spice: Cook the recipe as written for a medium curry. If you prefer a mild curry, start with 2 tablespoons of curry paste. If you find yourself with a curry that's way too hot, you can add additional coconut cream or add vegetable/chicken stock.

Substitutions: Substitute zucchini and green beans with 3 cups of any suitable vegetables such as snow peas, sugar snap peas, broccoli, broccolini, capsicum or baby corn. If you don't like fish, you can use thinly sliced chicken breast or thigh instead. Add the chicken breast in at step 4 before you add the veggies. Give it 10 minutes to poach in the coconut cream before adding the beans and zucchini.

Right Round, Baby

Week 8

Sunday

Pan-Fried Lamb Yiros

Monday

Keftedes and Risoni Bake

Tuesday

Chicken and
Cauliflower Tikka Masala

Wednesday

Simple Tuna Spaghetti

Thursday

Chicken and
Cauliflower Tikka Masala

Friday

Buttermilk Chicken Burgers

Saturday

Hoisin Lettuce Cups

Week 8 at a Glance

★ Servings: 28
plus 6 leftovers

★ $2.49
per serve

By now you may have realised that I have an ongoing love affair with meatballs! If I had to pick one variety to eat for the rest of my life it would be keftedes (Greek meatballs). For a simple meal, I serve them up with a fresh Greek salad and roasted lemon potatoes, but in this week's plan you'll be making Big Mac taco style Pan-Fried Lamb Yiros and my easy Keftedes and Risoni Bake.

Sunday

Of all the meals on this plan, the Pan-Fried Lamb Yiros excites me the most. The flavours are just SO good! Take the time earlier in the day to make the Simple Flatbreads and homemade Tzatziki. It really adds to the flavour and you'll have to trust me that it's 100 per cent worth the extra effort. Half of the keftedes mixture (Greek meatballs) is used for this recipe and you'll keep the other half for tomorrow night's dinner. If you have the time tonight, roll up the meatballs and pop them in the fridge, otherwise you can do it during prep tomorrow.

Monday

Tonight, you'll use the other half of the keftedes mixture to make this hearty Keftedes and Risoni Bake. You'll take it from stovetop to oven so I recommend using a large ovenproof frying pan or a cast iron French pan. Alternatively, you could start it on the stove in a frying pan and transfer it into a baking dish. If you want to stretch it further or feel as though you need more veg, I'd do some steamed greens or sautéed silverbeet as a side. For something lighter, make a basic Greek salad.

Tuesday

We're making a double batch of one of my favourite curries tonight. The Chicken and Cauliflower Tikka Masala isn't an exact replica of your Indian takeaway standard, but I've tried to stay true to the familiar flavours of this mild-medium creamy curry. Serve with basmati rice and pop your leftovers into the fridge for a night off cooking on Thursday. Cook a double batch of rice if you'd prefer to reheat the rice also. Although I don't usually encourage you to freeze dishes containing cream, this one does freeze very well.

Wednesday

Your hump day meal this week is so low-fuss. A slightly elevated version of a dish I lived off for a good 6 months when I was 19, this Simple Tuna Spaghetti is exactly what it claims to be. If you don't like tinned tuna, you could easily swap this recipe with the Green Carbonara in the Week 9 plan, without breaking the budget.

Thursday

Tonight is leftover night. You'll be heating up the extra servings of Tuesday's Chicken and Cauliflower Tikka Masala. If you didn't make extra rice on Tuesday, that's all you'll have to cook now to get dinner on the table. You might even want to make a batch of Simple Flatbreads, char them a little in the frying pan and brush with melted butter ... voilà, a simplified naan bread! I'd also recommend marinating the chicken tonight for tomorrow night's burgers, so they have plenty of time to bathe in the buttermilk.

Friday

I don't think I need to say much about the Buttermilk Chicken Burgers except that I wish I could have snuck in a jar of pickles under budget, because for me they're essential. However, I do realise that not everybody is a fan, so I'll leave that up to you! Pick a few lettuce leaves off the baby gem lettuces that you're using for tomorrow's dish or just serve up the coleslaw. I love a spicy mayo with this burger – I usually mix 1 part sriracha to 4 parts mayo for the sauce.

Saturday

We have another fast meal for an easy Saturday night dinner with these Hoisin Lettuce Cups. The protein you use is completely up to you. I usually choose pork mince, just because it's the cheapest! It is quite a light meal, so you could look at adding an additional side and/or some steamed jasmine rice if your family is ravenous.

WEEK 8

Week 8 Grocery List

Ingredients in italics are Pantry Staples (page 11), so you may have them already.

Meat and Fish

- 1 kg lamb mince
- 500 g chicken or pork mince
- 2 chicken breast fillets (500–600 g)
- 750 g boneless chicken thighs

Fruit and Veg

- 2 red onions
- 4 brown onions
- 3 bulbs garlic
- 50 g fresh ginger
- 1 bunch mint
- 1 bunch parsley
- 1 large carrot
- 2-pack little gem lettuce
- 1 iceberg or cos lettuce
- 5 large tomatoes
- 3 lemons
- ½ large cauliflower (500 g)
- 200 g bag coleslaw mix
- 1 large zucchini
- 1 Lebanese cucumber

Fridge and Freezer

- 150 g Greek feta
- 300 ml thickened cream
- 1 kg *plain Greek yoghurt*
- 2 *eggs*
- *unsalted butter*
- *milk*

Pantry

- garam masala
- 2 × 400 g tins diced tomatoes
- 700 g bottle passata
- 500 g risoni
- 500 g spaghetti
- 1 × 425 g tin of tuna in oil
- 4 burger buns
- hoisin sauce
- 1 × 225 g tin water chestnuts
- *olive oil*
- *extra virgin olive oil*
- *vegetable oil*
- *salt*
- *pepper*
- *paprika*
- *dried oregano*
- *ground cumin*
- *garlic powder*
- *ground turmeric*
- *ground coriander*
- *cayenne pepper*
- *dried chilli flakes*
- *brown sugar*
- *caster sugar*
- *dark soy sauce*
- *sesame oil*
- *tomato paste*
- *mayonnaise*
- *white vinegar*
- *panko breadcrumbs*
- *basmati rice*
- *chicken stock cubes/powder*
- *cornflour*
- *plain flour*
- *self-raising flour*

Week 8 Swap 'n' Save

Some weeks the budget is tighter than others, or you're more busy, more tired, have unexpected guests, want to mix things up, or are catering for dietary preferences. Use the tips below to vary your week accordingly.

Swap out

lamb mince ⟶ **pork or beef mince**

chicken breast ⟶ **4 boneless chicken thighs**

spaghetti ⟶ **any pasta shape**

little gem lettuce ⟶ **any soft lettuce**

Pocket some savings

Feta: Purchase feta from the deli at the supermarket unless you're going to use more than 150 g in the near future. The deli usually stocks Australian and Danish feta. The Australian variety is closest in texture to Greek feta so it's the better option. The price per kg is usually about the same as the home brand packaged feta and the deli regularly runs sales.

Mince: Pork mince is about $5 per kg cheaper than lamb mince so that's an easy $5 saving. I have made keftedes many times with combinations of beef, pork and lamb mince and prefer the lamb but would definitely choose pork/beef when my budget is tight.

Water chestnuts: Tinned water chestnuts are usually found in the Asian food aisle near the tinned baby corn and bean sprouts. They're a Chinese vegetable that are grown in marshes, underwater, and have quite a neutral taste with a little bit of a tang. They're a great addition to stir-fries for texture. If you have trouble finding a tin, it's not essential – just substitute finely sliced or diced mushrooms or capsicum.

Leftovers

You'll buy garam masala (Indian spice blend) this week for the Chicken and Cauliflower Tikka Masala. Use the leftover spices for the Spinach and Potato Curry in Week 9.

Pan-Fried Lamb Yiros

A Greek spin on 'Big Mac tacos'

Keftedes mixture

1 kg lamb mince
½ large red onion, grated or
   very finely chopped
4 cloves garlic, crushed
¼ cup mint leaves, finely chopped
¼ cup flat-leaf parsley leaves,
   finely chopped
2 teaspoons dried oregano
2 teaspoons salt
½ teaspoon ground black pepper
2 eggs, beaten
1½ cups (110 g) panko breadcrumbs

Yiros

1 quantity Simple Flatbreads
   and Tzatziki (page 173)
½ lettuce, finely sliced
3 large tomatoes, sliced
½ red onion, thinly sliced
olive oil, for cooking

To serve

crumbled feta
mint leaves
lemon wedges

PREP

✓ In a large bowl, add the ingredients for the **keftedes mixture** and combine well with your hands (gloves optional!) for a couple of minutes. Split the mixture in half, keeping half in the bowl for tonight's meal and putting the other half in the fridge for the **Keftedes and Risoni Bake**.

✓ Prepare and cook **Simple Flatbreads and Tzatziki** (next recipe).

✓ Finely slice the lettuce, tomatoes and red onion.

✓ Spread a thin layer (2–3 tablespoons) of the **keftedes mixture** onto **simple flatbread**.

COOK

1. Heat 1 tablespoon oil in a large frying pan over medium-high heat.

2. Add 2 or 3 yiros (lamb-topped **flatbread**) into the pan, meat side down and let them cook for 2–3 minutes or until browned. Flip them over and cook bread-side down for 1–2 minutes, until lightly browned, then remove from the pan. Repeat in batches until all of the yiros (18 in total) are cooked.

3. Top each yiros with lettuce, a couple of slices of tomato and a generous dollop of **tzatziki**.

4. Sprinkle with feta and mint, and serve 3 per person with a wedge of lemon on the side.

NOTES

Leftovers: Any uncooked **keftedes mixture** can be frozen for 1–2 months or stored in the fridge for 2 days (check the best before date of the mince first).

Meal plan: If you're following the meal plan, you'll have enough mixture to make the yiros and tomorrow night's

Keftedes and Risoni Bake. If you're making this as a standalone recipe for 4, just halve the quantities in the **keftedes mixture**.

Shortcut: Buying pre-made tzatziki and mini flatbreads will cut down a lot of the prep time. I recommend making

your own if you can though, particularly the tzatziki, because the store-bought version just doesn't compare!

Substitutions: Use pork mince, beef mince or a 50/50 pork and beef mince combo instead of lamb.

Simple Flatbreads and Tzatziki

Two of my go-to make from scratch sides

Flatbread

2 ¼ cups (335 g) self-raising flour, plus extra for dusting
1 ½ cups (420 g) plain Greek yoghurt
½ teaspoon salt

Tzatziki

1 Lebanese cucumber, grated, liquid strained
1 cup (280 g) plain Greek yoghurt
1 small garlic clove, crushed
2 teaspoons lemon juice
2 teaspoons extra virgin olive oil
¼ teaspoon salt
1 tablespoon finely chopped mint leaves

PREP

✓ For the flatbread, combine the flour, yoghurt and salt in a large mixing bowl. Stir well with a spoon then use your hands to gather it into a large ball of dough.

✓ Lightly dust flour on a clean benchtop or large wooden board and transfer the dough onto it. Divide in half, then in half again and continue portioning it until you have 18 evenly sized portions. Roll each portion into a ball with your hands and set aside. Allow the dough to rest for 5–10 minutes while you make the tzatziki.

✓ To make the tzatziki, coarsely grate the cucumber and drain out as much liquid as possible in a metal strainer or by wringing it out in a clean tea towel, then add to a bowl.

✓ Add the rest of the tzatziki ingredients to the bowl, stir well to combine then cover and chill until you're ready to serve.

COOK

1. Heat a non-stick frying pan over medium-high heat. You can use a small amount of oil but I prefer to cook them in a dry pan. While it's heating up, use a rolling pin to flatten the dough balls into thin 12 cm rounds (or use your hands to stretch out the dough). You'll need to add about a teaspoon of additional flour to each ball to prevent them from sticking.

2. Cook 1 or 2 flatbreads at a time (depending on the size of your pan) for about 1–2 minutes each side, until lightly browned. Serve warm or store at room temperature in an airtight container for up to 3 days.

WEEK 8

Keftedes and Risoni Bake

Greek meatballs baked on a bed of pasta

½ quantity (about 3 cups)
   keftedes mixture (page 170)
½ large zucchini, diced
1 brown onion, diced
3 cloves garlic, crushed
3 tablespoons olive oil
2 tablespoons tomato paste
1 tablespoon dried oregano
2 × 400 g tins diced or crushed
   tomatoes
3 ½ cups (875 ml) chicken stock
500 g risoni
1 teaspoon salt
¼ teaspoon ground black pepper
juice of ½ lemon

To serve
100 g feta, crumbled
2 tablespoons parsley, finely chopped
lemon wedges (optional)

PREP

✓ Preheat the oven to 170°C.

✓ Roll slightly heaped tablespoons of the **keftedes mixture** into balls. Set aside on a plate or cover and refrigerate if prepping ahead.

✓ Dice the zucchini and onion and crush the garlic.

COOK

1. Heat 2 tablespoons oil in a large ovenproof frying pan over medium-high heat.

2. Cook the meatballs in batches for a few minutes until they are browned all over, then transfer to a plate. They will finish cooking in the oven later.

3. Remove any leftover charred meatball remnants from the pan, reduce the heat to medium and add remaining oil to the pan. Add the zucchini and onion and cook, stirring, for 4–5 minutes, until soft.

4. Add the garlic and stir for 1 minute then add the tomato paste, stirring through. Add the oregano, diced tomatoes, chicken stock and risoni and bring to a gentle simmer, stirring occasionally. Stir in the salt and pepper.

5. Once the mixture is simmering, spread the risoni out evenly then gently place the meatballs into the sauce. Carefully transfer the pan onto a rack in the lower half of the oven, uncovered, and bake for 20 minutes. When it's ready, the risoni should be al dente.

6. Squeeze lemon juice over the risoni and divide among bowls or serve family-style at the table. Sprinkle with feta and parsley. Serve with lemon wedges, if using.

NOTES

Dairy-free: Omit the feta.

Leftovers: Store in the fridge for up to 3 days. This dish can be frozen for 1 month but is best eaten fresh or reheated in the microwave or stovetop.

Chicken and Cauliflower Tikka Masala

You'll have this curry on regular rotation!

SERVES 8

PREP 15 minutes + marinating time
COOK 40 minutes

Spice mix
2 tablespoons garam masala
2 teaspoons paprika
1 teaspoon ground cumin
1 teaspoon ground turmeric
1 teaspoon ground coriander
1 teaspoon salt
¼ teaspoon cayenne pepper

Chicken marinade
750 g boneless chicken thighs
2 cloves garlic, crushed
2 teaspoons finely grated fresh ginger
⅓ cup (95 g) plain Greek yoghurt
½ quantity spice mix
    (about 2 tablespoons)

Curry
2 brown onions, finely diced
3 cloves garlic, crushed
1 tablespoon finely grated fresh ginger
½ large cauliflower (500 g)
4 tablespoons vegetable oil
2 tablespoons unsalted butter
½ quantity spice mix
    (about 2 tablespoons)
2 teaspoons salt
2 tablespoons tomato paste
700 g bottle passata
1 tablespoon caster sugar
300 ml thickened cream

To serve
steamed basmati rice
plain Greek yoghurt or leftover
    Tzatziki (page 173)
pappadums or a half serve of the
    Simple Flatbreads (page 173),
    brushed with melted butter (optional)

PREP

✓ Combine the spice mix ingredients together in a small bowl.

✓ Crush the garlic and grate the ginger for the chicken marinade. Cut the chicken thighs into 3–4 cm cubes.

✓ Place the garlic, ginger, yoghurt and 2 tablespoons of the spice mix into a large bowl and stir together, then add chicken and coat in the marinade. Refrigerate for a minimum of 1 hour or up to overnight. Keep the remaining spice mix for later.

✓ Chop or break the cauliflower into florets, similar in size to the chicken pieces.

✓ When you're ready to cook the curry, take the marinated chicken out of the fridge, dice the onion, crush the garlic and grate the ginger.

COOK

1.   Heat a large pot or your largest frying pan over medium-high heat and add 1 tablespoon oil. Cook chicken in 2 or 3 batches until browned well on each side, topping up the oil as necessary with each batch. Transfer to a plate.

2.   Wipe the pan clean, turn heat down to medium and heat 2 tablespoons butter and 1 tablespoon oil. Add onions and about ½ teaspoon salt. Cook for 4–5 minutes, stirring.

3.   Add garlic and ginger to the pan and stir for a minute. Add the reserved spice mix and stir through the onion mixture for 30 seconds, then add the tomato paste. Cook for another minute then add the passata, 1 cup (250 ml) water and remaining salt. Bring to a gentle simmer. This is a good time to start cooking your rice.

4.   Add the cauliflower, turn down heat to medium-low and simmer, partially covered, for 15 minutes or until the cauliflower is tender.

5.   Add the chicken to the sauce mixture then stir in the sugar and cream. Gently simmer for another few minutes. Taste and add salt or more sugar to balance the flavours.

6.   Serve over steamed basmati rice, with yoghurt or tzatziki, and pappadams or simple flatbreads on the side.

NOTES

Chicken: This can be made with chicken breast but chicken thighs will be far more juicy and flavoursome.

Leftovers: Store in the fridge for up to 2 days. Freeze for 1 month and reheat on the stovetop or in the microwave.

Spice: I would place this curry at the upper end of 'mild'. If you'd like a little more spice, just increase the amount of cayenne pepper to ½ –¾ teaspoon. If you find this too spicy, just add in a bit of extra cream or stir through some yoghurt.

Simple Tuna Spaghetti

For those nights where you just want to take it easy

500 g spaghetti
425 g tin tuna in oil, drained
½ red onion, diced
4 cloves garlic, crushed
1 tablespoon lemon juice
1 tablespoon extra virgin olive oil
1 teaspoon dried chilli flakes
1 tablespoon finely chopped flat-leaf
   parsley leaves

To serve
finely grated zest of 1 lemon
finely chopped flat-leaf parsley leaves

PREP

✓ Put a large pot of salted water on to boil.

✓ Drain the excess oil from the tuna.

✓ Dice the onion and crush the garlic. Zest the lemon and finely chop the parsley.

COOK

1. Once the water is boiling, add the spaghetti.

2. When the spaghetti is about halfway cooked, heat the oil in a large frying pan over medium heat and add the onion. Cook for a few minutes, until soft and translucent. Add the garlic and chilli flakes and cook, stirring, for 30 seconds.

3. Add the tuna and lemon juice into the pan and stir through. If the spaghetti is not yet ready, take it off the heat.

4. When the spaghetti is ready, scoop out ½ cup of pasta water and set aside. Drain the spaghetti in a colander then add it into the frying pan with the tuna. Mix it through well, add the parsley and a generous amount of freshly ground pepper and salt to taste.

5. Divide among bowls and top with lemon zest and extra parsley.

NOTES

Flavour boost: For something a little more fancy, add capers or anchovies. I prefer this without parmesan but my kids like to add it – give it a try!

Leftovers: This can be stored for 3 days in the fridge and reheated in the microwave or on the stovetop but it's best served immediately after cooking. This recipe is not suitable for freezing.

Buttermilk Chicken Burgers

Succulent, crispy-coated chicken

SERVES 4

PREP 25 minutes + 3 hours marinating

COOK 20 minutes

2 chicken breast fillets (500–600 g)
vegetable oil, to fry

Buttermilk marinade
1 cup (250 ml) milk
1 tablespoon white vinegar
2 teaspoons salt
½ teaspoon paprika
½ teaspoon cayenne pepper

Coating
2 cups (300 g) plain flour
2 teaspoons baking powder
1 teaspoon salt
1 teaspoon paprika
¾ teaspoon ground black pepper
½ teaspoon garlic powder
½ teaspoon cayenne pepper
5 tablespoons buttermilk marinade

Coleslaw
1 tablespoon finely chopped flat-leaf
    parsley leaves
200 g coleslaw mix
2 teaspoons white vinegar
¼ cup (75 g) mayonnaise

Burger
4 burger buns, halved
2 tomatoes, sliced
4 large lettuce leaves
mayonnaise or sriracha mayo

PREP

✓ To make the buttermilk marinade, combine the milk and vinegar in a shallow bowl or container. Stir and set aside for 5 minutes to separate (curdle). Add the salt, paprika and cayenne pepper and stir together.

✓ Cut chicken breast in half horizontally. Add chicken to the marinade, cover and refrigerate for 1 hour or up to 24 hours.

✓ Remove the chicken from the fridge. Mix the flour, baking powder, salt, paprika, black pepper, garlic powder and cayenne pepper together in a shallow bowl. Add 5 tablespoons of the marinade sauce to the coating mixture, stirring loosely together until even clumps of the dry mix are spread throughout.

✓ Place the marinated chicken pieces into the coating mixture and turn to coat well on both sides. Transfer to a plate or tray.

✓ Chop parsley and add to a medium bowl with the coleslaw mix. Stir through the vinegar, mayonnaise and a pinch of salt. Cover and refrigerate for later.

✓ Halve the burger buns and slice the tomato.

COOK

1. Preheat the grill to toast the burger buns (optional). Fill a large deep pan with at least 5 cm of oil. Heat over high heat until hot, then reduce heat to medium-high. The oil should be about 180°C.

2. Fry the chicken in the oil for 8–10 minutes, turning with tongs once the bottom side is golden brown. Remove to a plate and drain on paper towel. Depending on the size of your pan you may need to cook in batches.

3. Toast the burger buns (buttered or plain) on a tray under the grill, cut side up, for about 30 seconds.

4. Assemble the burgers by spreading a thick layer of mayonnaise on both buns. On the bottom bun stack a lettuce leaf, a piece of fried chicken, tomato slices and coleslaw. Place the bun lid on top.

NOTES

Buttermilk: The milk and vinegar combination is a homemade version of buttermilk. This can be used in cakes, pancakes or any recipe that calls for buttermilk.

Frying: You can use a deep fryer but you'll use a lot more oil. I prefer to shallow fry in a pot or large wok and top up the oil if necessary. Any flavourless oil that's suitable for frying can be used. You can also strain and funnel your oil into a jar/bottle and reuse next time you're frying chicken.

Hoisin Lettuce Cups

A fresh explosion of flavour in each bite!

Sauce
⅓ cup (80 ml) hoisin sauce
2 tablespoons dark soy sauce
2 teaspoons caster sugar
1 teaspoon sesame oil
1 teaspoon cornflour

Stir-fry
2 cloves garlic, crushed
1 teaspoon finely grated fresh ginger
1 brown onion, finely diced
½ large zucchini, finely diced
225 g tin water chestnuts,
    drained and finely chopped
1 tablespoon vegetable oil
500 g chicken or pork mince

To serve
2 little gem lettuces, leaves separated
1 large carrot, cut into thin
    matchsticks or grated
sliced green onion (optional)
mint leaves

PREP

✓ Combine **sauce** ingredients with 2 tablespoons water in a bowl or jug. Mix and set aside.

✓ For the **stir-fry** component, crush the garlic and grate the ginger. Dice the onion, dice the zucchini. Drain and finely chop the water chestnuts.

✓ Cut carrot into thin matchsticks or coarsely grate. Separate the lettuce leaves and arrange them onto plates.

COOK

1. Heat a wok or large frying pan over high heat then add the oil.

2. When the oil is hot, add the onion and cook for a minute. Stir in the garlic and ginger for 10 seconds then add the mince, breaking it up and stir-frying until mostly browned. This should take about 5 minutes.

3. Add the water chestnuts and zucchini to the pan, cook for another minute or two. Give the sauce a quick stir, pour it into the pan and stir through to coat everything.

4. Stir-fry for another couple of minutes, until sauce has thickened. Taste and add a little extra sugar or soy sauce if you'd like a little more sweetness or salt.

5. Spoon the mixture into the lettuce leaves and top with carrot, green onions and mint to serve.

NOTES

Gluten-free: Use tamari or gluten-free soy sauce and make sure the hoisin sauce is gluten-free.

Leftovers: Store leftover stir-fry in the fridge for 2 days. Reheat it in the microwave or the wok. I don't recommend freezing this dish.

Substitutions: Beef mince can be used instead of pork or chicken mince. Any finely diced vegetables can be added to the stir-fry to bulk up the dish or add more colour.

Quick and Simple

Week 9

Sunday
Spicy Pork Ramen

Monday
Green Carbonara

Tuesday
Spinach and Potato Curry

Wednesday
Tomato Soup

Thursday
Spinach and Potato Curry

Friday
Asian Glazed Drumsticks

Saturday
Creamy Tomato Rigatoni

Week 9 at a Glance

 **28 meals**
plus 1 leftover

 $2.40
per serve

This is one of my simplest, cheapest meal plans with four of this week's recipes ready in under 30 minutes. We also have four nights of meat-free meals, my favourite of which is the veg-packed **Spinach and Potato Curry**.

Sunday

The ease with which you cook tonight's **Spicy Pork Ramen** depends entirely on how well you prep. Ensure that you read the recipe and prep steps first because timing is everything. You'll have three pots and pans on the stovetop simultaneously to boil the eggs, simmer the stock and stir-fry the pork. It sounds a lot more complicated than it is, though! Go easy on the sriracha when seasoning the pork because the spice will seep into the stock and heat up the entire dish. You can always add extra chilli sauce into your bowl after serving.

Monday

This **Green Carbonara** is pretty on the plate, delicious to eat and effortless to prepare. When asparagus is in season, you can substitute it for the broccolini. This is a meal I often make when my kids aren't home and I need to use up remnants of veggies in my crisper. I also serve this up for guests with garlic bread and a simple rocket, parmesan and pear salad – low fuss entertaining at its best.

Tuesday

I always feel so nourished after eating my **Spinach and Potato Curry**. You'll be making a double batch (8 servings) so you'll have leftovers to eat later in the week. Serve it with basmati rice and pappadams. It's not a spicy curry – I'd class it as 'mild' but it does have a little kick. Just leave out the cayenne if you're concerned about the spice levels. You can also add more coconut milk or cream to tone down the spice for sensitive palates. Make extra rice tonight if you want less work on Thursday.

Wednesday

Tonight's **Tomato Soup** made from tinned tomatoes is one of my go-to recipes when I'm feeling under the weather. It's comforting, low-effort and I usually have all of the ingredients on hand. It's almost mandatory to serve this with some kind of bread and my favourite is the **Cheesy Parmesan Toast**. Make sure that you save the other half of the passata for Saturday's **Creamy Tomato Rigatoni**.

Thursday

Tonight is leftover night and all you have to do is reheat the **Spinach and Potato Curry**. Serve it with basmati rice and pappadams which can be cooked in the microwave or fried. Like most curries, I always think this tastes better when it's reheated a day or two later.

Friday

Who doesn't love sticky, sweet and salty **Asian Glazed Drumsticks**?! You can prepare the accompaniments – steamed jasmine rice and Asian greens – while the drumsticks are in the oven. This recipe is so easy to scale up or down whether you're cooking for a crowd or just cooking for one or two people. Don't forget to drizzle the glaze over *everything*!

Saturday

The sauce for this **Creamy Tomato Rigatoni** is ready in the time it takes to cook the pasta, so on a good day I can have this on the table in just 15 minutes. It's the type of pasta dish that my family inhales in record time but it's deceptively filling. If you would like to serve it with sides, I'd suggest a simple green salad and/or garlic bread.

Week 9 Grocery List

Ingredients in italics are Pantry Staples (page 11), so you may have them already.

Meat and Fish

- 500 g pork mince
- 8 chicken drumsticks (about 1.5 kg)
- 100 g bacon

Fruit and Veg

- 1 kg potatoes
- 1 bunch green onions
- 3 brown onions
- 2 bulbs garlic
- 50 g fresh ginger
- 1 carrot
- 1 small zucchini
- 1 bunch broccolini
- 1 small bunch baby bok choy
- 1 large bunch bok choy
- 1 lemon
- 1 bunch basil

Fridge and Freezer

- 300 ml thickened cream
- 2 × 250 g packets frozen spinach
- 180 g frozen peas
- *parmesan cheese*
- *unsalted butter*
- *9 eggs*

Pantry

- *garam masala*
- 2 × 400 g tins whole peeled tomatoes
- 1 × 400 g tin diced or crushed tomatoes
- 1 × 700 g bottle passata
- 1 × 400 g tin chickpeas
- 1 × 400 ml tin coconut milk
- 500 g fettuccine
- 500 g rigatoni
- 5 × 85 g (single serve) nests instant noodles
- 1 pack pappadams
- *olive oil*
- *vegetable oil*
- *salt*
- *pepper*
- *ground turmeric*
- *ground cumin*
- *ground coriander*
- *dried oregano*
- *cayenne pepper*
- *dried chilli flakes*
- *brown sugar*
- *caster sugar*
- *jasmine rice*
- *basmati rice*
- *light soy sauce*
- *oyster sauce*
- *rice wine vinegar*
- *sesame oil*
- *sriracha*
- *cornflour*
- *vegetable stock cubes/powder*
- *tomato paste*
- *honey*
- *sesame seeds*
- *1 loaf thick sliced white bread*

Week 9 Swap 'n' Save

Some weeks the budget is tighter than others, or you're more busy, more tired, have unexpected guests, want to mix things up, or are catering for dietary preferences. Use the tips below to vary your week accordingly.

 Swap out

pork mince ⟶ chicken mince

bacon ⟶ pancetta

frozen spinach ⟶ baby spinach or silverbeet

chickpeas ⟶ brown lentils

fettuccine ⟶ spaghetti or linguine

rigatoni ⟶ penne

passata ⟶ crushed tomatoes

$ Pocket some savings

Asian veg: Check out your local Asian grocer for Asian vegetables. They're often far cheaper than supermarkets and more generous in size.

Home brand: Save by choosing home brand pasta and tinned goods. However if you have a little extra in the budget, splurge on better quality whole peeled tomatoes for the soup. They're a little less acidic and fuller flavoured.

Chicken: Compare prices with the chicken drumsticks. Often 2 kg bags can be a similar price to buying 1.5 kg at the deli. If so, freeze the extra drumsticks or use them to make the **Chicken Soup** in Week 1.

Noodles: The cheapest option for the ramen (and one you might already have handy!) is a 5-nest pack of home brand instant noodles which is around $2. I usually cook all 5 nests, ditch the seasoning and divide them between 4 bowls. However, you can use any thin egg noodle for the soup. You'll need about 300 g dry noodles.

🖰 Leftovers

You'll have about 50 ml of thickened cream left this week as you'll only use 1 cup (250 ml) for the **Creamy Tomato Rigatoni**. You'll also have 2 egg whites after cooking the **Green Carbonara**. Why not throw them into an omelette or some ultra creamy scrambled eggs? You could also use up the additional cream by swirling it through the tomato soup.

Spicy Pork Ramen

Deliciously zingy noodle soup

5 × 85 g (single serve) nests
    instant noodles

Stock

6 cups (1.5 litres) chicken stock
2 teaspoons light soy sauce
2 cloves garlic, smashed
2 cm piece fresh ginger, thinly sliced
2 green onions (pale parts),
    roughly sliced

Pork

1 tablespoon vegetable oil
1 brown onion, finely diced
2 cloves garlic, crushed
1 teaspoon finely grated fresh ginger
500 g pork mince
2 tablespoons light soy sauce
2 teaspoons oyster sauce
1 tablespoon brown sugar
½–1 teaspoon sriracha

Toppers

4 eggs
1 small bunch baby bok choy,
    halved lengthways
½ bunch broccolini, halved crossways
green onions (dark green part),
    thinly sliced
1 carrot, peeled and cut into
    matchsticks
dried chilli flakes

PREP

✓ Smash 2 cloves of garlic for the **stock** and crush another 2 for the **pork**. Slice a 2 cm piece of ginger for the stock and grate 1 teaspoon for the pork.

✓ Finely dice the brown onion, roughly slice the pale part of the green onion and thinly slice the dark green part. Peel and cut the carrots into thin matchsticks.

COOK

1. Add water to a small saucepan and bring to the boil over medium-high heat. Turn the heat down to medium, gently lower in the eggs and set a timer for 6 minutes. Once the timer goes off, remove the eggs from the pan and place in a bowl of very cold or iced water.

2. While the water for the eggs is coming to the boil, add all of the stock ingredients to a larger saucepan. Bring to the boil then reduce heat to low and keep at a simmer, partially covered.

3. For the **pork**, heat a large frying pan or wok over medium-high heat. Add the oil and onion. Stir-fry for 3 minutes then add the garlic and ginger, cooking for another minute.

4. Add pork mince and turn the heat up to high. Cook, stirring, until pork mince is browned. Add soy sauce, oyster sauce and sugar and allow the pork mince to caramelise a little. Add sriracha, ½ teaspoon at a time, tasting until it reaches the right level of spice for you, then turn off the heat.

5. Add the broccolini and bok choy to the stock and cook for 2–3 minutes. While this is cooking, prepare the noodles according to packet instructions, drain and set aside. Peel and halve the eggs.

6. Divide the noodles between 4 bowls with the bok choy and broccolini, ladle about a cup of stock into each bowl then top with pork, 2 egg halves and carrots. If you want it to be more 'soupy' add in extra stock. Serve topped with green onions and chilli flakes.

NOTES

Eggs: If you'd prefer hard-boiled eggs, set your timer for 8 minutes. It's important that you transfer them into cold water immediately once the timer goes off to prevent them from cooking further.

Leftovers: Any leftover cooked pork mince can be stored in the fridge for 3 days and served over rice.

Noodles: You can use mie goreng, instant ramen or any packaged noodles of your choosing.

Stock: You can strain the stock just before step 5 if you wish. I find that it's quite easy to avoid serving up the aromatics (ginger, garlic, etc.) if I'm careful when I ladle it.

Timing: When you cook this for the first time, it may seem a little fiddly with 3 separate pots and pans on the stove at once. I recommend reading the recipe through a couple of times before you get started because it all comes together quite quickly. When you cook it next, it'll be a walk in the park!

Green Carbonara

Traditionally cream-free with some nutritious additions

3 whole eggs (yolk and white)
  + 2 egg yolks, beaten
2 cloves garlic, crushed
⅔ cup (50 g) finely grated parmesan
100 g bacon, sliced into thin pieces
  or diced
½ bunch broccolini,
  cut crossways into 3–4 pieces
1 small zucchini, thinly sliced
500 g fettuccine
1 teaspoon olive oil
¾ cup (90 g) frozen peas

To serve
juice of ½ lemon
shaved parmesan

PREP

✓ Bring a large pot of salted water to the boil over high heat.

✓ In a medium bowl or jug, beat the eggs. Crush the garlic, grate the parmesan (if not pre-grated) then add in with the eggs, whisk together and set aside.

✓ Slice the bacon, broccolini and zucchini.

COOK

1. Once the water is boiling, add the fettuccine.

2. Meanwhile, heat oil in a large frying pan over medium heat. Add the bacon and cook for 3–4 minutes or until it just starts to become crisp. Add the zucchini and broccolini stems, cooking for a few minutes, stirring. Add in the broccolini florets and the peas and cook for another couple of minutes then move the pan off the heat until you're ready to serve.

3. When the pasta is about a minute away from perfection, scoop out 1 cup of pasta water, set it aside then drain the pasta in a colander.

4. Transfer the drained pasta back into the now empty pot it was cooked in (off the heat). Pour the egg and cheese mixture into the pasta and stir through to combine, adding in a little pasta water at a time to help enhance the creaminess.

5. Toss the bacon and greens gently through the mixture, adding a little more pasta water to ensure that it's not too dry. Divide among bowls or plates. Add a good squeeze of lemon juice, season with pepper and top with shaved parmesan.

NOTES

Leftovers: Any leftovers can be stored in the fridge for 2 days and reheated in the microwave or on the stovetop. I usually keep the extra egg whites to add to scrambled eggs or omelettes the next morning. Don't throw them away!

Pasta: Use any pasta – my preferred choices for this recipe are linguine, fettuccine and spaghetti.

Spinach and Potato Curry

A tasty, well-balanced Indian veg dish

Spice mix

1 tablespoon garam masala
2 teaspoons ground cumin
1 teaspoon ground turmeric
1 teaspoon ground coriander
1 teaspoon salt
¼ teaspoon cayenne pepper

Curry

1 kg potatoes, peeled and
    cut into 4 cm chunks
2 × 250 g packets frozen spinach,
    thawed
1 brown onion, diced
3 cloves garlic, crushed
1 teaspoon finely grated fresh ginger
2 tablespoons vegetable or olive oil
400 g tin diced or crushed tomatoes
400 ml tin coconut milk
1 cup (250 ml) vegetable stock
400 g tin chickpeas, rinsed and drained
¾ cup (90 g) frozen peas
1–2 teaspoons caster sugar
juice of ½ lemon

To serve

steamed basmati rice
pappadams

PREP

- ✓ For the **spice mix**, combine ingredients together in a small bowl.
- ✓ Start bringing a large pot of salted water to the boil over high heat.
- ✓ Peel the potatoes, cut them into 4 cm chunks and put them straight into the pot of water.
- ✓ Put the spinach in a sieve, run warm water over it until it thaws, press as much liquid out as possible then set aside.
- ✓ Dice the onion, crush the garlic and grate the ginger.

COOK

1. Parboil the potatoes for about 10 minutes or until just tender, then drain in a colander and set aside. If you're serving with rice, start cooking it now.

2. Meanwhile, heat oil in a large frying pan over medium heat. Add the onion and cook for 4–5 minutes, stirring occasionally, until soft. Add the garlic and ginger and cook for another minute or so.

3. Add the **spice mix** to the pan and cook, stirring, for 1 minute. Add the drained potatoes. Turn the heat up to medium-high and stir to coat the potatoes in the spices for a couple of minutes.

4. Add the diced tomatoes, coconut milk and vegetable stock. Bring to a simmer then turn the heat down to medium-low and cook, uncovered, for 10 minutes. Stir through the chickpeas, spinach and frozen peas with 1 teaspoon sugar and the lemon juice.

5. Taste and add a little more sugar and/or salt if necessary.

6. Divide among bowls with the steamed rice, and serve with pappadams.

NOTES

Leftovers: Store this in the fridge for 4 days or the freezer for 2–3 months. Reheat in the microwave or on the stovetop.

Substitutions: Use baby spinach, kale or silverbeet in place of the frozen spinach. A tin of brown lentils could be added in place of the chickpeas.

Tomato Soup

With buttery, cheesy parmesan toast

SERVES 4
PREP 10 minutes
COOK 20 minutes

1 brown onion, diced
3 cloves garlic, crushed
50 g unsalted butter
1 tablespoon dried oregano
2 × 400 g tins whole peeled tomatoes
350 ml passata (or another tin of tomatoes)
1 cup (250 ml) vegetable stock
12 large basil leaves
1 teaspoon caster sugar, if needed

Parmesan toast
¼ cup (60 g) unsalted butter, softened
¼ cup (20 g) finely grated parmesan
4 thick slices white bread

To serve
basil leaves

PREP

✓ Dice the onion and crush the garlic.

COOK

1. Melt the butter in a saucepan over medium-low heat then add the onion. Cook, stirring occasionally, for 5–10 minutes. You don't want them to brown, just become translucent and soft.

2. Add the garlic and dried oregano and stir for 1 minute.

3. Add tomatoes, passata and stock. Break up the tomatoes with a wooden spoon. Raise heat to medium- high and bring to a gentle boil, then turn heat to low.

4. Cover and simmer for 10–15 minutes, up to 30 minutes if you wish.

5. While the soup is simmering, combine the butter and parmesan for the **parmesan toast**. Spread it onto the bread. Heat a non-stick frying pan over medium heat. Cook the bread, butter-side down, for a couple of minutes or until it is lightly golden. Repeat with the remaining bread, then cut each slice in half.

6. Remove the soup from the heat, taste and season with salt and pepper. Stir through the basil leaves. Add a teaspoon of sugar if it tastes a little acidic.

7. Blend the soup with a stick blender until smooth. Divide among bowls, top with basil leaves and serve with the parmesan toast.

NOTES

Dietaries: For dairy-free, replace the butter in the soup with 2 tablespoons olive oil and replace the butter and parmesan on the bread with a drizzle of olive oil. For gluten-free, use gluten-free bread.

Leftovers: Store in the fridge for 4 days and reheat on the stovetop or in the microwave. This soup can be frozen for 2 months.

Parmesan toast: The quantities I've listed for the butter and parmesan are quite conservative so if you, like me, love the idea of ultra cheesy, buttery toast – double it!

Asian Glazed Drumsticks

A family-friendly Friday night favourite

INGREDIENTS

8 chicken drumsticks (about 1.5 kg)
1 large bunch bok choy
1 tablespoon cornflour

Glaze
3 cloves garlic, crushed
¼ cup (60 ml) light soy sauce
¼ cup (60 ml) honey
2 tablespoons brown sugar
1 tablespoon oyster sauce
1 teaspoon rice wine vinegar
1 teaspoon sesame oil

To serve
steamed jasmine rice
sesame seeds
green onions, sliced

PREP

✓ Preheat the oven to 190°C. Line a large baking tray with baking paper.

✓ Crush the garlic then add it into a small saucepan along with the soy sauce, honey, brown sugar, oyster sauce, rice wine vinegar and sesame oil for the **glaze**.

COOK

1. Heat the glaze ingredients over low heat until sugar has dissolved and the ingredients are evenly combined. Turn off the heat.

2. Put the chicken in a large bowl and coat it well with about ¼ cup (60 ml) of the glaze. Leave the rest in the saucepan on the stove. Arrange the chicken pieces on the baking tray, grind some pepper over them and pop the tray on a rack in the middle of the oven.

3. Cook for 40–45 minutes, brushing them with a little more glaze after about 30 minutes. While the chicken is baking, cook the rice and steam the bok choy.

4. Once you've glazed the chicken, mix the cornflour with 1 tablespoon water in a small bowl to make a slurry. Add it into the saucepan with the remaining glaze. Heat on low, stirring until the sauce thickens to a consistency that will stick to the chicken.

5. When the chicken is ready, remove it from the oven. Brush with about half the thickened glaze (or use a spoon to drizzle it over) and sprinkle with sesame seeds and green onions.

6. Serve with steamed jasmine rice and bok choy. Drizzle the remaining glaze over the bok choy.

NOTES

Bok choy: I halve the bok choy lengthways and steam it for about 5 minutes, covered. Select the largest bundle you can find at the supermarket or grocer.

Chicken: Cook as many drumsticks as your family will eat. You can also use maryland, wings or skin-on chicken thighs for this recipe.

Glaze: Feel free to double the glaze quantity if you want it to be extra saucy. I find that this amount is perfect for my family of 4.

Gluten-free: Replace the soy sauce with tamari or gluten-free soy sauce, and make sure the oyster sauce is gluten-free.

Leftovers: Store in the fridge for 2 days and reheat in the microwave. Freeze the drumsticks for up to 2 months.

Creamy Tomato Rigatoni

Low-effort, pretty plate of pasta

3 cloves garlic, crushed
¼ cup (20 g) finely grated parmesan
500 g rigatoni (tube pasta)
3 tablespoons unsalted butter
350 ml passata
1 tablespoon tomato paste
1 cup (250 ml) thickened cream
1 teaspoon dried oregano
½ teaspoon dried chilli flakes

To serve
¼ cup basil leaves, thinly sliced
finely grated parmesan

PREP

✓ Bring a large pot of salted water to the boil over high heat.

✓ Crush the garlic and grate the parmesan.

COOK

1. Cook the rigatoni in the boiling water until almost al dente.

2. Melt the butter in a large frying pan over low heat. Add the garlic and stir for a minute.

3. Stir in the passata, tomato paste, cream, oregano, chilli flakes and half the parmesan. Gently simmer on low for 5 minutes.

4. Season the sauce with salt and freshly ground black pepper to taste, and add additional oregano, chilli flakes or parmesan if you wish.

5. When the rigatoni is about a minute away from perfection, scoop out ½ cup of pasta water and drain the pasta in a colander.

6. Add the pasta to the pan with the sauce and stir through. If the sauce is a bit thick add in some pasta water to help distribute it.

7. Divide among bowls and top with parmesan and basil, with extra pepper if you like.

NOTES

Leftovers: Store in the fridge for 3 days and reheat in the microwave. I don't recommend freezing this dish.

Pasta: Use any pasta shape for this recipe. Penne is a great substitute for rigatoni.

Summer Lovin'

Week 10

Sunday
Pulled Pork Burgers

Monday
Thai Pineapple Fried Rice

Tuesday
Chicken, Chickpea
and Feta Salad

Wednesday
Loaded Sweet Potatoes

Thursday
Cheat's Pad Thai

Friday
Chorizo, Spinach and Feta Pasta

Saturday
Soy Hokkien Noodles

Week 10 at a Glance

 **28 meals**
plus 7 leftovers

 $2.48
per serve

This week's star is the **Slow Cooked Pineapple Pulled Pork**. Whether you choose to cook it in the oven or your slow cooker, it's pretty much foolproof and will be the base of 3 meals this week: **Pulled Pork Burgers**, **Thai Pineapple Fried Rice** and **Loaded Sweet Potatoes**.

Sunday

Ensure that you allow yourself enough time to slow cook the pork for tonight's **Pulled Pork Burgers**. To be safe, you'll need about 4 ½ hours prep and cook time if you're using the oven. For the slow cooker I'd allow 5 ½ hours total if you're cooking it on high and 10 hours if you're cooking it on low. You'll probably have to stop yourself from picking at the leftovers after you've made the burgers but you will need to set aside at least 1 cup pulled pork for the **Thai Pineapple Fried Rice** and 2 cups for the **Loaded Sweet Potatoes**.

Monday

I used to preach that fried rice should only be made with day-old, cool rice but I've since changed my stance. I've made this **Thai Pineapple Fried Rice** many times, using rice I've cooked just half an hour prior and it's delicious every time. If you do have the time, you can dry it out a little by spreading the cooked rice out on a plate and popping it in the fridge for 15+ minutes, uncovered. If not, don't stress! Throw any extra veg you have into this to add colour and crunch.

Tuesday

Tonight's **Chicken, Chickpea and Feta Salad** is a light summery weeknight meal that will still leave you feeling satisfied. You'll be marinating the chicken in the same spice mix as the **Middle Eastern Chicken and Rice** from Week 4 – big pops of flavour using your pantry staple spices. To bulk this up for bigger appetites, you can always increase the amount of chicken to 150–200 g per person.

Wednesday

Most of the cook time for tonight's **Loaded Sweet Potatoes** is hands-off which makes it a pretty simple mid-week dinner. You can customise the topping if you wish but the classic pulled pork, coleslaw and sour cream combo is delish.

Thursday

Pad thai purists might shake their heads at my **Cheat's Pad Thai** but I really can't justify asking you to buy a jar of tamarind paste for this one dish! You still have the sour, sweet, salty elements of a traditional pad thai as well as the crunch from the fresh bean sprouts and crushed peanuts. Change up the protein if you're sick to death of chicken but it will always be my first choice for this Thai restaurant classic.

Friday

This **Chorizo, Spinach and Feta Pasta** is one of my go-to meals when my planning has gone off the rails (it happens to the best of us!) and I have 5 minutes to grab the ingredients for a cheap, last-minute dinner. It's tasty, quick, filling and it has chorizo . . . need I say any more?!

Saturday

Tonight's **Soy Hokkien Noodles** are classic Chinese takeaway-style noodles, and like most stir-fries, incredibly versatile. Pick your choice of protein and veggies – you can't go wrong! I've chosen baby corn and choy sum but don't feel limited to these. As with the fried rice, you can easily throw in another cup or so of chopped veggies if you're wanting to bulk up the meal or avoid waste.

Week 10 Grocery List

Ingredients in italics are Pantry Staples (page 11), so you may have them already.

Meat and Fish

- 1.8 kg boneless pork shoulder roast
- 1 chorizo sausage (125–150 g)
- 1.1–1.2 kg chicken breast

Fruit and Veg

- 1 bunch green onions
- 4 brown onions
- 3 large tomatoes
- 3 Lebanese or 2 continental cucumbers
- 3 bulbs garlic
- 1 large bunch choy sum or bok choy
- 4 sweet potatoes (about 250 g each)
- 2 limes
- 3 lemons
- 1 red capsicum
- 120 g baby spinach
- 1 bunch coriander
- 2 × 200 g bags coleslaw mix
- 250 g bean sprouts

Fridge and Freezer

- sour cream
- 150 g feta cheese
- 9 eggs

Pantry

- barbecue sauce
- 6 burger buns
- 2 × 400 g tins cherry tomatoes
- 1 × 425 g tin pineapple slices in juice
- 500 g penne
- 2 × 200 g packets dried wide rice noodles
- 2 × 400 g packets shelf-fresh hokkien noodles
- 1 × 150 g packet crushed peanuts
- 2 × 400 g tins chickpeas
- 1 × 410 g tin baby corn
- *olive oil*
- *extra virgin olive oil*
- *vegetable oil*
- *salt*
- *pepper*
- *garlic powder*
- *paprika*
- *ground cumin*
- *ground coriander*
- *ground cinnamon*
- *ground turmeric*
- *dried oregano*
- *cayenne pepper*
- *dried chilli flakes*
- *brown sugar*
- *caster sugar*
- *jasmine rice*
- *light soy sauce*
- *dark soy sauce*
- *oyster sauce*
- *rice wine vinegar*
- *sesame seeds*
- *sriracha*
- *fish sauce*
- *cornflour*
- *chicken stock cubes/powder*
- *vegetable stock cubes/powder*
- *tomato paste*
- *mayonnaise*
- *white vinegar*

Week 10 Swap 'n' Save

Some weeks the budget is tighter than others, or you're more busy, more tired, have unexpected guests, want to mix things up, or are catering for dietary preferences. Use the tips below to vary your week accordingly.

 Swap out

chicken breast $\longrightarrow$ boneless chicken thigh

continental cucumbers $\longrightarrow$ Lebanese cucumbers

sweet potatoes $\longrightarrow$ regular potatoes

penne $\longrightarrow$ rigatoni

bok choy $\longrightarrow$ any Asian greens

800 g fresh hokkien noodles $\longrightarrow$ 400 g any dried noodles

tinned cherry tomatoes $\longrightarrow$ tinned crushed or diced tomatoes

💲 Pocket some savings

Coleslaw: You can make your own coleslaw mix by shredding red or green cabbage and carrot. Compare the prices to see which option is the best value.

Chorizo: Always look for the chorizo at the deli counter first as it's often half price. Chorizo can be frozen for up to 3 months.

Crushed peanuts: The crushed peanuts are for the **Cheat's Pad Thai**.

Burger buns: The cheapest option for bread rolls/burger buns is almost always the 6 packs in the major supermarkets.

Choices, choices

Noodles: For the **Cheat's Pad Thai**, I recommend thin flat rice noodles. Substitute the thin flat rice noodles with thick flat rice noodles if you can't find them, usually labelled as pad thai noodles. For the **Hokkien Soy Noodles**, I recommend fresh, shelf stable hokkien noodles that usually come in 400 g packs or the fresh, refrigerated noodles. These can be replaced with any egg noodle, however if you're using dry noodles, you'll only need 400–500 g.

Burger buns: Unpopular opinion – I know that pulled pork burgers are usually served with brioche buns but I really don't like the sweetness of the brioche, layered with the sweetness of the barbecue pork. I prefer a plain burger bun that lets the flavours of the pork and coleslaw shine. It's completely up to you but keep this in mind.

🍱 Leftovers

If you cook the meal plan as written, the only ingredient you'll have remaining (aside from pantry items) is barbecue sauce. Chances are this is a staple for you, so I'm sure you'll find a use for it!

Slow Cooked Pineapple Pulled Pork

Juicy, sweet, shredded meat

SERVES 8–10
PREP 15 minutes
COOK 3 hours 45 minutes

1.8 kg pork shoulder
1 large brown onion, diced
2 cloves garlic, crushed
425 g tin pineapple slices in juice
2 tablespoons vegetable oil
⅔ cup (160 ml) barbecue sauce
¼ cup (55 g) brown sugar
1 teaspoon salt
1 teaspoon pepper

PREP

✓ Preheat the oven to 140°C.

✓ Trim and discard the skin and any excess fat from the pork shoulder. Cut the meat into 5 or 6 large pieces. Season all sides well with salt and freshly ground black pepper.

✓ Dice the onion and crush the garlic.

✓ Drain the juice from the pineapple tin into a bowl and dice 2 of the slices. Put the remaining slices in the fridge, reserved for the **Thai Pineapple Fried Rice**.

COOK

1. Heat 1 tablespoon oil in a large pan (cast iron is ideal) over medium-high heat. Cook the pork in 2 batches, turning to brown on each side, about 7 minutes for each batch. Transfer to a plate once browned.

2. Add a little more oil to the pan if needed, reduce the heat to medium and add the onion. Cook, stirring occasionally, for a few minutes until soft then add the garlic, pineapple juice, diced pineapple, barbecue sauce, brown sugar, salt and pepper. Bring the mixture to a simmer then turn off the heat.

3. If you're using a cast iron pan or Dutch oven, add the pork into the pan, put the lid on and transfer to the oven. If you used a frypan to brown the pork, transfer the sauce and the pork into an ovenproof baking dish and cover with a lid or a layer of baking paper topped with a layer of foil.

4. Roast for 3 hours. Remove the dish from the oven and use a fork to test the pork. If it pulls away with minimal resistance and is very tender, it's ready. If not, let it cook for another 30 minutes.

5. When ready, shred the pork with 2 forks, removing any large pieces of fat. Stir the pork through the sauce to coat it well. Taste and season with salt, pepper or more brown sugar if necessary.

NOTES

Leftovers: Store in the fridge for up to 3 days. Reheat in the microwave or on the stovetop in a frypan. Freeze for 2 months.

Meal plan: If cooking as part of the meal plan, reserve 2 cups of the pulled pork for the **Loaded Sweet Potatoes**, 3 cups for the **Pulled Pork Burgers**, and the remainder for the **Thai Pineapple Fried Rice** along with the leftover pineapple slices.

Slow Cooker: Transfer to a slow cooker at step 3 and cook for 4–5 hours on high or 8–9 hours on low.

Pulled Pork Burgers

Eating these might get a little messy ... but so worth it!

Coleslaw
200 g coleslaw mix
2 tablespoons mayonnaise
2 tablespoons sour cream
2 teaspoons white vinegar
1 teaspoon caster sugar

Burger
3 cups Slow Cooked Pineapple
   Pulled Pork (page 208)
6 burger buns, halved
mayonnaise, to taste
barbecue sauce, to taste

PREP

✓ Tip the coleslaw into a medium bowl. Stir through the mayonnaise, sour cream, vinegar, sugar and a pinch of salt.

✓ Halve the burger buns and preheat the grill to toast them.

✓ Heat up the pulled pork in a frying pan or microwave if it's no longer warm.

COOK

1. Toast the burger buns (buttered or plain) on a tray under the grill, cut side up, for about 30 seconds.

2. Assemble the burgers by spreading a thick layer of mayonnaise on both buns. On the bottom bun, stack the coleslaw, a generous amount of pulled pork and barbecue sauce. Top with the burger bun lid. Serve immediately.

NOTES

Leftovers: If you're only cooking for four, I recommend making the extra two burgers the next day to send in school or work lunches.

Thai Pineapple Fried Rice

A light but punchy dish

SERVES 5
PREP 10 minutes
COOK 10 minutes

2 cups (400 g) jasmine rice
  (6 cups cooked)
1–1½ cups **Slow Cooked Pineapple
  Pulled Pork** (page 208)
5 eggs, lightly beaten
1 brown onion, diced
4 cloves garlic, crushed
1 red capsicum, diced
4–5 slices tinned pineapple, drained
  and thinly sliced
1½ tablespoons vegetable oil

Stir-fry sauce
3 tablespoons fish sauce
2 tablespoons light soy sauce
2 teaspoons brown sugar
1 teaspoon sriracha (optional)

To serve
coriander, chopped
green onions, sliced
lime wedges

PREP

- ✓ If you're not using pre-cooked rice, cook the rice now.
- ✓ Chop the pulled pork into smaller pieces. Beat the eggs in a small bowl.
- ✓ Dice the brown onion, crush the garlic, dice the capsicum, and slice the pineapple.
- ✓ For the **stir-fry sauce**, combine the fish sauce, soy sauce, brown sugar and sriracha in a bowl or jug.

COOK

1. Heat ½ tablespoon oil in a wok or large frying pan over medium-high heat. Add the eggs and cook, stirring, until softly scrambled. Transfer to a plate or bowl, and wipe the wok clean.

2. Turn the heat up to high, add remaining 1 tablespoon oil then add the onion and capsicum. Stir-fry for 1–2 minutes, until starting to soften, then add the garlic and stir-fry for another minute.

3. Add the rice and **stir-fry sauce**. Stir-fry for a few minutes to heat through, then add the egg back in along with the pork and stir through well.

4. Taste and add extra fish sauce or soy sauce for a stronger salty flavour, or chilli for more heat (be careful it doesn't get too salty). Add the pineapple and stir through.

5. Divide among bowls, top with coriander and green onions and serve with lime wedges.

NOTES

Gluten-free: Use tamari or gluten-free soy sauce.

Leftovers: Store in the fridge as soon as possible after cooking, for up to 2 days. Reheat in a wok or pan with 1 tablespoon oil for best results and ensure that it is piping hot before serving, particularly because you'll be reheating the pork (and potentially the rice) for the second time. I don't recommend freezing fried rice.

Rice: As a general rule, 1 cup of uncooked rice = 3 cups cooked rice. I used to preach that you should only use leftover cold rice for fried rice, but most of the time I use freshly cooked rice. If you have the time, allow it to dry out for 10–15 minutes while you prep by spreading it out on a tray or large plate and popping it in the fridge, uncovered.

Substitutions: You can substitute the leftover pork for cooked chicken, prawns or tofu.

Chicken, Chickpea and Feta Salad

Make extra and take it to work the next day!

SERVES 4
PREP 20 minutes
COOK 10 minutes

Marinated chicken
400 g chicken breast fillet
2 teaspoons lemon juice
1 clove garlic, crushed
2 tablespoons olive oil
1 teaspoon ground cumin
1 teaspoon ground coriander
½ teaspoon paprika
½ teaspoon ground turmeric
½ teaspoon salt
¼ teaspoon cayenne pepper
⅛ teaspoon ground cinnamon

Salad
3 Lebanese cucumbers or 2 continental
  cucumbers, sliced
3 tomatoes, cut into wedges
2 green onions, thinly sliced
⅓ cup coriander leaves, chopped
100 g feta, crumbled
2 × 400 g tins chickpeas,
  rinsed and drained

Dressing
¼ cup (60 ml) extra virgin olive oil
¼ cup (60 ml) lemon juice
1 tablespoon chopped coriander leaves
1 large clove garlic, crushed
½ teaspoon caster sugar
½ teaspoon salt

To cook
1 tablespoon olive oil

PREP

✓ Slice the chicken breast in half horizontally.

✓ Juice the lemon and crush the garlic for the marinade and dressing.

✓ Mix **marinade** ingredients together in a bowl or shallow dish then add chicken and stir well to coat with the marinade. Set aside whilst prepping the salad or cover and refrigerate to marinate for longer.

✓ Mix the **dressing** ingredients together in a small bowl and set aside.

✓ To make the **salad**, slice the cucumber and cut the tomato into wedges, slice the green onions, chop the coriander and add to a large salad bowl. Crumble the feta into the salad, drain and rinse the chickpeas and add them in also. Drizzle the dressing over the salad and season generously with salt and freshly ground pepper. Toss gently to combine.

COOK

1. Heat 1 tablespoon of olive oil in a frying pan over medium-high heat. Transfer the marinated chicken breasts to the pan and cook for 4–5 minutes on each side or until they are golden brown and cooked through.

2. Remove from the pan and slice into thin strips. Divide the salad and chicken among bowls and serve warm.

NOTES

Dairy-free: Omit the feta.

Leftovers: Store this in the fridge for 2 days. The chicken can be frozen for up to 2 months. Reheat the chicken in the microwave or serve cold with the salad.

Substitutions: Boneless chicken thighs can be used in place of the chicken breast.

Loaded Sweet Potatoes

Comforting, filling, delicious!

SERVES 4
PREP 10 minutes
COOK 1 hour 15 minutes

Coleslaw
200 g coleslaw mix
2 tablespoons mayonnaise
2 tablespoons sour cream
2 teaspoons white vinegar
1 teaspoon caster sugar

Loaded potatoes
4 small sweet potatoes
(about 250 g each)
1–2 tablespoons olive oil
1–2 teaspoons salt
2 cups Slow Cooked Pineapple
Pulled Pork (page 208)

To serve
sour cream
green onions, sliced

PREP

✓ Preheat the oven to 200°C. Line a shallow roasting tray with baking paper.

✓ Tip the coleslaw mix into a medium bowl. Stir through the mayonnaise, sour cream, vinegar, sugar and a pinch of salt. Cover and refrigerate until ready to serve.

✓ Wash sweet **potatoes** and dry well with a tea towel or paper towel (don't peel!).

✓ Use a fork to lightly poke holes in each potato 5 or 6 times.

✓ Place the potatoes on the lined tray. Rub or brush the skin all over with a light covering of olive oil then sprinkle with salt.

COOK

1. Place the tray on a rack in the middle of the oven and bake the potatoes for 60–75 minutes. The cooking time will depend on the size of the potato. The skin should be pretty crispy and you should be able to easily pierce the potatoes with a skewer or a knife. If in doubt leave them in another 5–10 minutes.

2. Just prior to removing the potatoes from the oven, reheat the pulled pork on the stovetop or in the microwave.

3. Carefully slice the potatoes from end to end, making sure that you don't cut all the way down to the bottom. You can use a fork to gently fluff up the insides if you wish.

4. Spoon the **coleslaw** then the **pulled pork** onto each sweet potato and top with a generous dollop of sour cream. Sprinkle with sliced green onion.

NOTES

Leftovers: There probably won't be any, but if you have leftover baked sweet potatoes, you can store them in the fridge for 3 days and reheat in the oven at 180°C for 15–20 minutes.

Potatoes: You can substitute any baking potato for the sweet potato.

Cheat's Pad Thai

Same sweet and tangy flavour, slightly different ingredients!

Sauce
¼ cup (60 ml) fish sauce
¼ cup (60 ml) rice wine vinegar
⅓ cup (75 g) brown sugar
2 tablespoons light soy sauce
1–2 teaspoons sriracha

Stir-fry
300 g chicken breast fillet, thinly sliced
400 g dried wide rice noodles
4 eggs, beaten
½ brown onion, thinly sliced
3 cloves garlic, crushed
2 ½ tablespoons vegetable oil
250 g bean sprouts

To serve
coriander leaves
sliced green onions
crushed peanuts
lime wedges

PREP

✓ Slice chicken into thin strips and set aside.

✓ Mix **sauce** ingredients together in a bowl.

✓ Place dried noodles in a large bowl and cover with boiling water. Let them soften for about 10 minutes while you finish prep and start cooking. Check them regularly and once they are softened but al dente, drain in a colander.

✓ Beat the eggs in a small bowl.

✓ Dice the onion and crush the garlic.

COOK

1. Heat a wok or large frying pan over high heat then add 1 tablespoon oil.

2. When the oil is hot, add chicken and spread out over the bottom of the pan. Allow it to sear for a minute then stir-fry it for another minute or until cooked through. Remove from the pan and set aside on a large plate.

3. Heat 1–2 teaspoons oil (depending how much is left from the chicken) then tip in the beaten egg. Cook, stirring, until softly scrambled then transfer to the plate with the chicken.

4. Heat another tablespoon of oil. Stir-fry the onion and garlic for 30–60 seconds then turn the heat up to high. Add the noodles followed by the sauce. Toss gently for about a minute, to coat the noodles in the sauce.

5. Add the chicken and egg back into the pan with the bean sprouts. Stir gently to coat all of the ingredients with the sauce. Cook for another couple of minutes, stirring occasionally, to heat through.

6. Divide among bowls and top with coriander, green onions and chopped peanuts. Serve with lime wedges.

NOTES

Gluten-free: Use tamari or gluten-free soy sauce.

Leftovers: Store in the fridge for 2 days and reheat in the microwave or in the wok. I don't recommend freezing this dish.

Noodles: I prefer thin flat rice noodles for this dish but you can use any flat rice noodles labelled as pad thai noodles.

Protein: You can replace the chicken with tofu, beef, pork or prawns.

Chorizo, Spinach and Feta Pasta

A quick and tasty weeknight favourite

1 chorizo sausage, thinly sliced
1 brown onion, finely diced
4 cloves garlic, crushed
500 g penne
1 tablespoon olive oil
1 tablespoon tomato paste
1–2 teaspoons dried chilli flakes
(to taste)
2 × 400 g tins cherry tomatoes
1 chicken or vegetable stock cube,
crumbled
120 g baby spinach

To serve
50 g feta, crumbled

PREP

✓ Bring a large pot of salted water to the boil over high heat.

✓ Halve the chorizo lengthways then slice thinly.

✓ Dice the onion and crush the garlic.

COOK

1. Tip the pasta into the boiling water and cook until al dente.

2. Meanwhile, heat 1 tablespoon of olive oil in a large frying pan over medium heat. Add chorizo and cook for about 5 minutes or until browned, then transfer to a plate leaving the flavoured oil in the pan.

3. Add the onion and cook, stirring, for a few minutes until soft. Add the garlic and cook for another minute. Add tomato paste, stir through for 30 seconds then add chilli flakes, cherry tomatoes and crumbled stock cube.

4. Bring to a simmer and cook for a few minutes. Add chorizo back in with the spinach and stir gently until spinach wilts.

5. Drain the pasta, reserving ½ cup of pasta water. Add the pasta to the sauce and stir through. Turn off the heat and add ¼ cup of pasta water, adding more if you'd like a thinner consistency. Taste and season.

6. Divide among bowls and season with freshly ground pepper. Top with crumbled feta.

NOTES

Dietaries: For gluten-free, ensure that the chorizo does not contain gluten, and use gluten-free pasta. For dairy-free, omit the feta.

Leftovers: Any leftovers can be stored in the fridge for 3 days and reheated in the microwave or on the stovetop. I don't recommend freezing this dish.

Pasta: Use any pasta for this but my preferred choices for this recipe are penne and rigatoni.

Soy Hokkien Noodles

Deliciously saucy

SERVES 6
PREP 15 minutes
COOK 15 minutes

Marinade
400–500 g chicken breast fillet,
    thinly sliced (or diced)
2 teaspoons cornflour
1 tablespoon light soy sauce
¼ teaspoon ground black pepper
1 teaspoon vegetable oil

Sauce
¼ cup (60 ml) chicken stock
2 tablespoons dark soy sauce
2 tablespoons oyster sauce
1 tablespoon light soy sauce
1 teaspoon rice wine vinegar
1 tablespoon brown sugar
1 teaspoon cornflour

Stir-fry
800 g shelf-fresh hokkien noodles
3 cloves garlic, crushed
3 green onions, sliced (separate pale
    and dark green parts)
1 large bunch choy sum or bok choy,
    sliced
410 g tin baby corn, drained
3 tablespoons vegetable oil

To serve
sliced dark green onions
sesame seeds

PREP

✔ Thinly slice the chicken. Add to a bowl with the rest of the **marinade** ingredients and mix to ensure that it is well coated. Set aside for 10 minutes while you prep the rest of the ingredients.

✔ Mix the **sauce** ingredients together in a medium bowl or jug then set aside.

✔ Prep noodles according to packet instructions.

✔ Crush the garlic and slice the green onion. Roughly slice the choy sum leaves and stalks then drain the baby corn.

COOK

1. Heat a wok over high heat and add 2 tablespoons oil. Cook the chicken, making sure you spread it out in the wok and let it sear on each side, then transfer to a plate. This should only take 1–2 minutes.

2. Heat another tablespoon of oil if necessary, then add the garlic and the pale parts of the green onion and stir-fry for 30 seconds.

3. Give the sauce a quick stir then add to the wok with the baby corn and choy sum. Cook for about a minute then add the chicken back into the wok and the noodles.

4. Stir-fry for at least a minute or until the sauce is coating the noodles, chicken and veggies – it should be thick and glossy.

5. Divide among bowls and top with sliced green onions and sesame seeds.

NOTES

Flavour boost: If you'd like an extra kick, a dash of sriracha in the last minute or two of cooking is delicious.

Noodles: I usually prepare the fresh noodles by putting them in a bowl of hot water and using my fingers to gently tease the noodles apart, without breaking them.

Protein: You can substitute the chicken with any protein. If using sliced beef, add ½ teaspoon bicarb soda into the marinade to tenderise it, and let it marinate for an extra 15 minutes.

Vegetables: Use any combination of stir-fry veg for this dish. Aim for 3–4 cups in total.

Index A–Z

Handy Index by Themes

Dairy-free and dairy-free option meals

Asian Glazed Drumsticks 199
Asian Slaw 45
Beef and Lentil Bolognese 161
Beef Burrito Bowls 109
Black Pepper Beef 113
Butter Bean Stew 98
Cheat's Pad Thai 219
Chicken, Chickpea and Feta Salad 215
Chicken Fried Rice 79
Chicken Lo Mein 138
Chicken Pad See Ew 118
Chicken Soup 34
Chicken Taco Soup 157
Chorizo and Lentil Soup 91
Chorizo, Spinach and Feta Pasta 221
Glazed Carrots 150
Greek Lemon Chicken and Potatoes 29
Greek Lemon Potatoes and
    Green Beans 29

Hoisin Lettuce Cups 182
Italian Meatball Sauce 67
Italian Wedding Soup 76
Keftedes and Risoni Bake 174
Korean Beef Bowls 158
Lamb Harira 134
Meatball Bánh Mì 49
Mexican Beef Chilli 20
Middle Eastern Chicken Marinade 95
Mongolian Beef 92
Pan-Fried Fish with Lemon Garlic Butter
    Sauce 72
Pork Noodle Stir-Fry 56
Rainbow Minestrone 24
Roasted Pumpkin Soup 137
Simple Tuna Spaghetti 178
Slow Cooked Greek Lamb 126
Slow Cooked Pineapple Pulled Pork
    208

Slow Cooker Mexican Beef 106
Smashed Potatoes 75
Soy Hokkien Noodles 222
Spanakorizo (Spinach Rice) 30
Spicy Pork Ramen 190
Spinach and Potato Curry 195
Thai Basil Chicken Stir-Fry 97
Thai Green Fish Curry 162
Thai Pineapple Fried Rice 212
Thai Red Chicken Curry 133
Tomato Soup 196
Twin Roast Chickens 146
Vegetable Massaman Curry 55
Veggie Tagine 117
Vietnamese Meatballs 42
Vietnamese Noodle Salad 154
Zingy Chicken Tray Bake 46

Fakeaway favourites

Beef Burrito Bowls 109
Beef 'n' Beans Nachos 114
Black Pepper Beef 113
Cheat's Pad Thai 219
Chicken Fried Rice 79

Chicken Lo Mein 138
Chicken Pad See Ew 118
Meatball Subs 71
Mongolian Beef 92
Pork Noodle Stir-Fry 56

Soy Hokkien Noodles 222
Thai Basil Chicken Stir-Fry 97
Thai Green Fish Curry 162
Thai Red Chicken Curry 133

Freeze for easy meals

Asian Glazed Drumsticks 199
Beef and Lentil Bolognese 161
Beef Chilli Mac 'n' Cheese 27
Butter Bean Stew 98
Buttermilk Fried Chicken 50
Chicken and Cauliflower
    Tikka Masala 177
Chicken, Chickpea and Feta Salad 215
Chicken Paprikash 110
Chicken Soup 34
Chicken Taco Soup 157
Chorizo and Lentil Soup 91
Cornbread Muffins 23

Italian Meatball Sauce 67
Italian Spaghetti Meatballs 64
Italian Wedding Soup 76
Keftedes 170
Keftedes and Risoni Bake 174
Lamb Harira 134
Mexican Beef Chilli 20
Middle Eastern Chicken Marinade 95
Rainbow Minestrone 24
Roast Chicken Gravy 153
Roasted Pumpkin Soup 137
Slow Cooked Greek Lamb 126
Slow Cooked Pineapple Pulled Pork 208

Slow Cooker Mexican Beef 106
Spinach and Potato Curry 195
Thai Green Fish Curry 162
Thai Red Chicken Curry 133
Tomato Soup 196
Twin Roast Chickens 146
Vegetable Frittata 68
Vegetable Massaman Curry 55
Veggie Mac 'n' Cheese 80
Veggie Tagine 117
Vietnamese Meatballs 42

Gluten-free and gluten-free option meals

Asian Glazed Drumsticks 199
Asian Slaw 45
Beef and Lentil Bolognese 161
Beef Burrito Bowls 109
Beef Chilli Mac 'n' Cheese 27
Beef 'n' Beans Nachos 114
Black Pepper Beef 113
Butter Bean Stew 98
Cheat's Pad Thai 219
Chicken and Cauliflower
   Tikka Masala 177
Chicken, Chickpea and Feta Salad 215
Chicken Fried Rice 79
Chicken Pad See Ew 118
Chicken Paprikash 110
Chicken Pesto Pasta 88
Chicken Soup 34
Chicken Taco Soup 157
Chorizo and Lentil Soup 91
Chorizo, Spinach and Feta Pasta 221
Creamy Mash 52

Glazed Carrots 150
Greek Lemon Chicken and Potatoes 29
Greek Lemon Potatoes and
   Green Beans 29
Hoisin Lettuce Cups 182
Italian Meatball Sauce 67
Italian Spaghetti Meatballs 64
Korean Beef Bowls 158
Lamb Harira 134
Loaded Potatoes 33
Loaded Sweet Potatoes 216
Mexican Beef Chilli 20
Middle Eastern Chicken Marinade 95
Mongolian Beef 92
Pan-Fried Fish with Lemon Garlic
   Butter Sauce 72
Rainbow Minestrone 24
Roasted Pumpkin Soup 137
Slow Cooked Greek Lamb 126
Slow Cooked Pineapple Pulled
   Pork 208

Slow Cooker Mexican Beef 106
Smashed Potatoes 75
Spanakorizo (Spinach Rice) 30
Spiced Lamb and Eggplant Farfalle 130
Spinach and Potato Curry 195
Thai Green Fish Curry 162
Thai Red Chicken Curry 133
Thai Basil Chicken Stir-Fry 97
Thai Pineapple Fried Rice 212
Tomato Soup 196
Twin Roast Chickens 146
Tzatziki 126, 173
Ultra Crispy Roast Potatoes 149
Vegetable Frittata 68
Vegetable Massaman Curry 55
Veggie Tagine 117
Vietnamese Meatballs 42
Vietnamese Noodle Salad 154
Zingy Chicken Tray Bake 46

Hot summer nights

Asian Glazed Drumsticks 199
Asian Slaw 45
Beef 'n' Beans Nachos 114
Black Pepper Beef 113
Buttermilk Fried Chicken 50
Cheat's Pad Thai 219
Chicken, Chickpea and Feta Salad 215

Chicken Lo Mein 138
Chicken Pad See Ew 118
Green Carbonara 193
Hoisin Lettuce Cups 182
Meatball Bánh Mì 49
Mongolian Beef 92
Pork Noodle Stir-Fry 56

Thai Basil Chicken Stir-Fry 97
Tzatziki 126, 173
Vegetable Frittata 68
Vietnamese Meatballs 42
Vietnamese Noodle Salad 154

Hungry: on the table in 30 minutes or less

Asian Slaw 45
Beef Chilli Mac 'n' Cheese 27
Beef 'n' Beans Nachos 114
Black Pepper Beef 113
Butter Bean Stew 98
Cheat's Pad Thai 219
Chicken, Chickpea and Feta Salad 215
Chicken Fried Rice 79
Chicken Lo Mein 138
Chicken Pad See Ew 118
Chicken Pesto Pasta 88

Chorizo, Spinach and Feta Pasta 221
Cornbread Muffins 23
Creamy Tomato Rigatoni 200
Hoisin Lettuce Cups 182
Italian Wedding Soup 76
Korean Beef Bowls 158
Meatball Bánh Mì 49
Meatball Subs 71
Mongolian Beef 92
Pan-Fried Fish with Lemon Garlic
   Butter Sauce 72

Pork Noodle Stir-Fry 56
Pulled Pork Burgers 211
Simple Tuna Spaghetti 178
Soy Hokkien Noodles 222
Spicy Pork Ramen 190
Thai Basil Chicken Stir-Fry 97
Thai Green Fish Curry 162
Tomato Soup 196
Vietnamese Meatballs 42
Vietnamese Noodle Salad 154

One pot wonders

Beef 'n' Beans Nachos 114
Butter Bean Stew 98
Chicken Lo Mein 138
Chicken Soup 34
Chicken Taco Soup 157
Chorizo and Lentil Soup 91
Chorizo, Spinach and Feta Pasta 221

Creamy Mash 52
Greek Lemon Chicken and Potatoes 29
Italian Wedding Soup 76
Keftedes and Risoni Bake 174
Lamb Harira 134
Meatball Subs 71
Mexican Beef Chilli 20

Middle Eastern Chicken Marinade 95
Rainbow Minestrone 24
Roasted Pumpkin Soup 137
Vegetable Frittata 68
Zingy Chicken Tray Bake 46

Sauces, dressings, condiments and more

Buttermilk Marinade 50, 181
Dipping Sauce (Vietnamese
    Meatballs) 42
Dressing (Asian Slaw) 45
Dressing (Chicken, Chickpea and

Feta Salad) 215
Fried Chicken Gravy 53
Italian Meatball Sauce 67
Pico de Gallo 109, 114
Roast Chicken Gravy 153

Slow Cooker Mexican Beef Dry Rub 106
Spice Mix, Mexican 46
Sriracha Mayo 49, 158
Tzatziki 126, 173
Yoghurt Sauce 130

Sidekicks: versatile side dishes

Cornbread Muffins 23
Creamy Mash 52
Garlic Bread 24
Glazed Carrots 150
Greek Lemon Potatoes and
    Green Beans 129

Loaded Potatoes 33
Simple Flatbreads 173
Smashed Potatoes 75
Spanakorizo (Spinach Rice) 30
Speedy Pickled Vegetables 49

Ultra Crispy Roast Potatoes 149
Vietnamese Noodle Salad 154

Vegetarian and vegetarian option meals

Asian Slaw 45
Butter Bean Stew 98
Cornbread Muffins 23
Creamy Mash 52
Creamy Tomato Rigatoni 200
Glazed Carrots 150
Greek Lemon Potatoes and

Green Beans 29
Italian Meatball Sauce 67
Rainbow Minestrone 24
Roasted Pumpkin Soup 137
Smashed Potatoes 75
Spanakorizo (Spinach Rice) 30
Speedy Pickled Vegetables 49

Spinach and Potato Curry 195
Tomato Soup 196
Ultra Crispy Roast Potatoes 149
Vegetable Frittata 68
Vegetable Massaman Curry 55
Veggie Mac 'n' Cheese 80
Veggie Tagine 117

Winter warmers

Beef and Lentil Bolognese 161
Butter Bean Stew 98
Chicken and Cauliflower
    Tikka Masala 177
Chicken Pesto Pasta 88
Chicken Soup 34
Chorizo and Lentil Soup 91
Creamy Tomato Rigatoni 200
Italian Meatball Sauce 67
Italian Spaghetti Meatballs 64

Italian Wedding Soup 76
Keftedes and Risoni Bake 174
Lamb Harira 134
Mexican Beef Chilli 20
Middle Eastern Chicken Marinade 95
Rainbow Minestrone 24
Roasted Pumpkin Soup 137
Slow Cooked Greek Lamb 126
Slow Cooked Pineapple Pulled
    Pork 208

Slow Cooker Mexican Beef 106
Spiced Lamb and Eggplant Farfalle 130
Spicy Pork Ramen 190
Spinach and Potato Curry 195
Thai Green Fish Curry 162
Thai Red Chicken Curry 133
Tomato Soup 196
Veggie Mac 'n' Cheese 80
Veggie Tagine 117

Acknowledgements

In March 2023 I opened a message in my inbox from Isabelle Yates which led to my cookbook dream becoming a reality. I want to start by saying a heartfelt thank you to Izzy for believing in me, supporting my vision and guiding me through this process with ease. Your capability and grace inspires me. I have truly loved working with you.

To the team at Penguin Random House, thank you all for your input and expertise in helping this evolve from concept to a published book that I'm so very proud of.

To my editor, Charle Malycon: you've taken what this first-time author has written and elevated it, one tweak and suggestion at a time, whilst still making me feel as though my voice is being heard – thank you.

To Tracy Rutherford, who has meticulously edited my recipes. Thank you, I appreciate your extensive knowledge and attention to detail.

I always wanted this book to be a beautiful book that you'd be excited to give or receive as a gift and I am so thankful to my book designer, Kirby Armstrong. Your creative interpretation of our vision for the book is just perfect.

This book wouldn't be what it is though without my photographer/food stylist extraordinaire, Melissa Darr. I don't have enough space on the page to adequately thank you for sharing your gift with me on this project but also for being a beautiful, kind human being. Your support throughout means so much, your photos are gorgeous – every single one – you should be so proud of your huge contribution to this book.

To Yvonne Curtis and Vanessa Curtis, who sliced, diced, washed an obscene amount of dishes and kept my spirits up during the shoots – thank you both. Your assistance and calm presence allowed me to relax, enjoy myself and keep my focus on cooking all of these recipes!

To my agent Grace Newman and the team at Ivy Talent Co: your guidance and experience has been invaluable and you've made me feel so comfortable knowing I'm in capable hands.

I owe all of this to my $10 Meals Australia Facebook community. How lucky am I to have grown a little patch in the social media landscape where people are kind, inclusive and supportive?! You've kept me going with your encouraging comments, private messages and the trust that you place in me every time you try a new recipe. This book is for all of you. Thank you so much.

To my fabulous recipe testing group who provided me with such detailed feedback: I appreciate and value every single one of you. Your responses have shaped this book for the better. Thank you.

To Sharyn, Cazz, Jodie and Maria: you have held down the fort moderating our $10 Meals community and given so much of your time. I am so grateful to each of you and so proud of what we have built together.

To my church family at Future Church: your support and encouragement means so much to me and my family. To Luke and Izumi Kennedy, my pastors: I want to thank you for building a spiritual home which fosters and encourages creativity.

To my wonderful friends/hype girls who have backed me every step of the way – I love you all and want to thank you for always being there for me. In particular, my friend and home cooking pro, Celina Chapman: you've been a much-needed sounding board and cheerleader, you've helped me retain my sanity (barely!) and I can't thank you enough.

Finally, to my beautiful children, Gabriel, Seth and Evie, my at-home taste testers, sous chefs, number one supporters and greatest motivation for pushing through. Thank you for allowing me the space and time to complete this book in record time. I love you all so much.

EBURY PRESS

UK | USA | Canada | Ireland | Australia
India | New Zealand | South Africa | China

Ebury Press is part of the Penguin Random House group of companies
whose addresses can be found at global.penguinrandomhouse.com

Penguin
Random House
Australia

First published by Ebury Press in 2024

Cover and internal photography by Melissa Darr © Penguin Random House Australia Pty Ltd
Cover and internal design by Kirby Armstrong © Penguin Random House Australia Pty Ltd
Food styling by Melissa Darr
Typeset in 9/12 pt Greycliff CF by Post Pre-press, Australia

Printed and bound in China by 1010 Printing International Ltd

 A catalogue record for this
book is available from the
National Library of Australia

ISBN 978 1 76134 451 0

penguin.com.au

*We at Penguin Random House Australia acknowledge that Aboriginal and Torres Strait Islander
peoples are the Traditional Custodians and the first storytellers of the lands on which we live
and work. We honour Aboriginal and Torres Strait Islander peoples' continuous connection
to Country, waters, skies and communities. We celebrate Aboriginal and Torres Strait Islander
stories, traditions and living cultures; and we pay our respects to Elders past and present.*